THROUGH THE
STORM

How To Lead When Things Go Bad

G. Paul Isaak

FriesenPress

Suite 300 - 990 Fort St
Victoria, BC, V8V 3K2
Canada

www.friesenpress.com

Copyright © 2017 by G. Paul Isaak
First Edition — 2017

ISBN
978-1-5255-1449-4 (Hardcover)
978-1-5255-1450-0 (Paperback)
978-1-5255-1451-7 (eBook)

1. SOCIAL SCIENCE, HUMAN SERVICES

Distributed to the trade by The Ingram Book Company

Dedicated to the memory of
Henry and Mary Buller;
to my life partner, Sylvia Buller Isaak
who held us all together during
the most tumultuous season of our lives;
and to our children,
Jessica and Hudson,
who have taught us to see
through the eyes of a child.

TABLE OF CONTENTS

7   **Preface**

11   **Chapter One –**

        Stepping up in a Time of Crisis

17   **Chapter Two –**

        Personal Crisis Defined

37   **Chapter Three –**

        Everyone Has a Story and Every Story Has its Time

47   **Chapter Four –**

        Three Responses When Bad Things Happen

63   **Chapter 5 –**

        The Paralyzing Misunderstandings of Stress

67   **Chapter 6 –**

        Common Signs and Symptoms of Distress

75   **Chapter 7 –**

        Why Me? The God Question

81   **Chapter 8 –**

        You're Not Crazy: Healthy Responses to Crisis

93   **Chapter 9 –**

        The Lie Everyone Wants You to Believe

101   **Regarding Chapter 10 and Chapter 11**

103   **Chapter 10 –**

        Taking Control of Your Life

109   **Chapter 11 –**

        Embracing the New You

115   **Appendix A**

PREFACE

Life is full of defining moments. Moments that take our breath away. Some of those moments bring joy and happiness beyond expression, such as the birth of a child. At the other end of the spectrum are moments that grip us in the pit of our stomachs, tragic circumstances that leave us with a sinking feeling of despair.

I will present material that equips leaders with a new understanding of what they can do when bad things happen in the lives of their staff. Significant research continues to take place in the areas of trauma, Post Traumatic Stress Disorder (PTSD), memory, how our brain records memories, and why memories impact us the way they do. Equal efforts continue to be made in identifying the most effective therapeutic treatment in assisting the victims of horrific events, the goal being to bring them back to healthy living. While this research must continue, any opportunities to prevent the debilitating effects of trauma must be given priority.

The material presented focuses on mitigating the need for professional support by equipping the leader with enough understanding of critical life-changing events that their genuine, timely, and meaningful support has a positive impact on the well-being and recovery of their staff.

News broadcasts detail the tragic circumstances that occur around us on a daily basis. Occasionally, we hear the stories of perseverance. In a Season Twelve episode of 'America's Got Talent', Kechi Okwuchi, one of only two survivors on board a 2005 Nigerian flight that crashed, killing 108, performed in front of a live and televised audience. The burn scars that cover sixty-five percent of her body did not stop her from performing as she sang her heart out and into the hearts of viewers around the world. We marvel at stories of resilience and breathe a collective sigh of relief that 'it was not us'. But the fact that some people thrive in the wake of a horrible event while others never recover highlights the need to understand what makes the outcomes so different. Quality living hangs in the balance.

Leaders in the workplace may not deal with the aftermath of an airplane crash, yet tragic circumstances, of varying degrees, do happen in the lives of their staff. Providing a genuine, meaningful, and supportive response to staff in a time of crisis can have lasting positive effect, impacting the relationship that employees have both to their boss and to the organization their boss represents.

The encouraging reality is that it is never too late to add a new skill set to your leadership toolbox.

Each and every one of us, particularly those in a place of influence, can be that difference maker to someone in the midst of a crisis. I have seen it happen, time and time again.

While my primary purpose in writing this book is to equip leaders with tools to support their staff during times of personal crisis, as this project evolved I envision its use in another capacity. Anyone in crisis will benefit from a greater understanding of what they are experiencing and the strategies that can assist them in their recovery in the days and weeks that follow. Providing knowledge and understanding to hurting people can be essential in their navigating through the rough waters that a crisis presents.

A significant portion of the material presented is orientated to the impacted person. The rationale for this and the language used is intended to assist the leader in empathizing with the very persons who require meaningful support. What grew out of this process is a framework for the impacted person to understand his or her experience combined with strategies to successfully navigate the challenges they face. Moving towards balanced and healthy living is a journey that is eased with valued assistance along the way. Leaders are critically positioned to be among those offering meaningful support.

CHAPTER ONE –
Stepping up in a Time of Crisis

Leadership training has historically focused on measuring performance, productivity, and efficiencies, and on creating a positive work environment, to name only a few points of emphasis. In more progressive environments leadership goes beyond performance and includes a focus on and commitment to the personal well-being of those who are part of their team. There is no greater time, nor is there a greater opportunity to focus on someone's well-being than in a time of crisis.

In the context of most leadership structures, you are a workplace leader if you hold the position of Chief Executive Officer (CEO), Chief Administrative Officer (CAO), Chair of the Board, Board member, President, Senior Vice-President, manager, or supervisor. Too often we limit our definition and understanding of leadership to those with lofty titles, perceived power and influence, by their physical location in the corner office, executive floor, or whatever space defines your organization's penthouse suite. Organizations are also impacted by seasoned and experienced employees who work alongside their peers in the trenches or front lines, employees whose opinions and actions matter. They are those employees who everyone pays attention to, noting their approval or disapproval of information presented by management. My reference to leaders will include not only those who are positioned within their organizational structure to lead, but also those who lead because it is in their very nature, character, and DNA to influence the world around them, regardless of their position or title. While positional leaders are advantaged, a true leader can surface almost anywhere.

Appointed leaders (CEO, Supervisors, Managers, etc.) are positioned to create a work environment where caring for one another naturally flows out of the respect, acceptance, and supportive relationships that should characterize every workplace. However, even in such an environment, knowing what to do and what to say to someone in the midst of a personal crisis is critical.

There is a notable difference between leading during times of organizational crisis and times of personal crisis. The skills needed in responding to a personal crisis are unique and are often not intuitive for those individuals who have advanced in the organizational structure. Instruction in this area is not often included in the traditional leadership training programs for those entering into the supervisory and management group. The chapters that follow are intended to fill that training gap.

While this leadership may not be intuitive, the encouraging news is that the tools needed can be learned when one is committed to what I refer to as higher goals; goals that focus on the personal well-being of their staff, recognizing that in doing so the organization is well served. Ironically, it is often the most unassuming individuals who naturally possess the wisdom and courage necessary to make a difference during these challenging and difficult circumstances.

I recently sat with a number of senior managers of an organization that had experienced a series of tragic circumstances that were impacting the workplace. The events, which culminated with the suicide of an employee whose life was spiraling downward, both professionally and personally, had left a mark on the organization. There were those who had worked alongside the employee questioning what they had missed. Supervisors, in particular, wondered if they had failed to see indicators of what was happening. Anger, betrayal, and outrage, along with other emotions such as sadness, guilt, and shame presented in one form or another. Overall morale, within the areas of the organization this employee had worked, was impacted by these tragic events.

I listened to their comments as they recalled conversations with those under their span of influence in the wake of this suicide. They seemed dissatisfied with how their conversations ended. It wasn't for a lack of motivation, or that their intentions were misguided in some way. They weren't. Their desire to do the right thing was real. These were good people who cared about their colleagues. They were simply lost about how to help. Unfortunately, when leaders are lost they can sometimes add to the feeling of despair felt by others in the organization. Worse yet, lost leaders can create a sense of alienation between themselves, who bear the burden of the organization's overall health, and those within the organization they are supposed to be supporting. Leading when things are going well is easy. When you have a strong team, one that understands its purpose, you just need to stay out of the way and cheer-lead from the sidelines. It is when things go bad that the value of strong, effective leadership is realized. In a crisis, leadership needs to be decisive. Those in leadership need to respond to the personal crisis with the same focus and intent as they would when faced with an organizational financial, marketing, or public relations crisis. They must have a clear picture of what the goal is and a game plan on how they are to reach their goal. Quarterbacks will have a much greater opportunity to achieve success if they know the playbook, and without that knowledge it is impossible for them to bring everyone together and working towards a common goal. Leaders who don't know what to do, don't know what say, or don't know how to respond following a personal crisis of someone in their sphere of influence will hurt their credibility in the areas where they actually have tremendous strengths. There is no greater time or opportunity to earn the trust and respect of your team than in a time of personal crisis.

It was the experience of talking with this group and others like it that highlighted the need to create a foundational resource on how to support those whose lives have been turned upside down; those who have experienced a tragic and life-changing event. Unfortunately, bad things happening to someone you know is as predictable as it is unavoidable. It is part of the life experience. The good news is that no life experience, good or bad, has the power to define who we are. These life experiences will surely shape who we are. It is our capacity to not only survive the bad things that happen to us, but to thrive in their aftermath that defines who we are. Resilience doesn't just happen. It happens when people are intentional. Keeping a dialogue open is closely connected to the development of resilience. Effective leaders find a way to make that happen.

The chapters that follow contain a blending of my professional and personal life experiences. In the professional context, I will draw from my training with the International Critical Incident Stress Foundation[1] and from my experience as the Winnipeg Police Service's Wellness Officer and Critical Incident Program

---

1 The International Critical Incident Stress Foundation (ICISF) provides leadership, education, training, consultation, and support services in areas of comprehensive crisis intervention and disaster behavioral health services to emergency response professions, other organizations, and communities worldwide.

Coordinator.[2] I held this position for seven years, during which time I met with 550 officers and their families in response to 189 Critical Incidents.

The privilege of interacting with those courageous men and women taught me a tremendous amount about human nature and the dynamics of tragic life circumstances. I am deeply thankful for the open and candid interactions that took place during that time.

In the personal context, my life journey is marked by a number of tragic circumstances that impacted my life. I experienced firsthand interactions with people who left me feeling hopeful that I could meet the challenges before me. I also experienced interactions with people who left me feeling tired, discouraged, and anything but hopeful. Being on the receiving end of genuine, meaningful, and supportive responses from individuals whose confidence was infectious was extremely powerful. In hearing the different parts of my story, you will be presented with examples of great leaders who impacted my life and helped to moved me through the storms that came along in my life's journey. Be encouraged and inspired by their example knowing that it is within each one of us to step up in a time of crisis.

---

2   The Wellness Officer position is a part of the Behavioural Health Services Unit of the Winnipeg Police Service. The Wellness Officer is responsible for the overall well-being and care of police and civilian members including their families, regardless of whether the critical events occurred in the workplace or not.

CHAPTER TWO –
Personal Crisis Defined

What does a personal crisis look like? The storms of life come in many shapes and sizes. No two storms are alike. I think we can all agree on a few obvious examples, such as the death of a loved one or diagnosis with a life-threatening illness. Things like 'unexpected loss' or 'cancer' clearly cross the threshold from 'everyday life experience' to 'personal crisis'.

Crisis in the most generalized state, however, is any experience that falls outside of a person's normal daily experience. The implication is that what constitutes a crisis for one individual may not in fact be a crisis for another. In my thirty-plus years as a police officer, and more specifically during my seven years as a Critical Incident Program Coordinator, I witnessed a wide range of responses to critical events. The diversity of an individual's professional and personal life experiences impacted on how an event was processed.

There are, however, markers that can generally be applied. Not surprisingly, the closer the relationship between us and the event, the more readily we see the situation as a personal crisis. The death of a husband, wife, or child is immediately accepted as a personal crisis, while the death of a second cousin or a distant uncle is more easily dismissed. We should, however, never assume how an event can or will impact another person.

From a leadership position, establishing a relationship with those who work within your span of influence is key to knowing when someone is in the midst of a personal crisis. This is not to suggest that you need to become everyone's best friend. I am referring to relationships characterized by trust and genuineness. Creating these kinds of relationships takes time and will require leaders to go beyond the traditional leadership skill set. You will likely find benefits beyond more congenial working conditions when you build these kinds of relationships. I have observed that leaders who focus on creating a genuine and trusting relationship with their employees often end up positively affecting their organization's bottom line. I have worked in a supportive and caring environment where my supervisors showed a genuine interest in me. They took time to ask questions about my family. As a result, they knew the names of my children. There is no doubt in my mind that that kind of relationship impacts an employee's contributions. Conversely, I have worked in an environment where there was little if any investment by my supervisors to get to know me. I like to think I rose above those circumstances but doing so takes a lot of energy to stay focused. Employees in such organizations tend to move on. When supervisors clearly show they care, one tends to give more of themselves in return. What is often observed is an increase in an employee's loyalty, commitment, and enhanced work satisfaction.

As the leader of the Forensic Services Unit, I provided oversight to career specialists and technicians, members who spent decades working in this particular field. Given the training investment and expertise necessary to do the work effectively, members who were transferred into the unit would often retire from the unit. I recall numerous conversations with one member about his decision to retire and all the considerations that went into the timing. After more than thirty-five years in the policing world, he was looking forward to retirement and to 'see the world' with his life partner. Within months of his retirement he suddenly found himself battling with cancer. Unfortunately, the battle ended before treatments even started. He passed away at sixty-four years of age. The many dreams he and his wife had for retirement were never realized. The impact of his death on his former coworkers could not have been more varied. It is critical for leaders to identify employees who may be quietly processing loss and pain in the immediate aftermath. To recognize and acknowledge that pain has a much greater impact than many people realize. Doing so communicates that you are paying attention, that you care about their well-being, and that you have enough courage to initiate a dialogue. Do not underestimate the value of a meaning-ful dialogue.

In my role as the Critical Incident Program Coordinator, I received a call early one morning from a supervisor who was concerned about the well-being of a young police officer on his shift. The officer and his partner had been involved in notifying the next of kin of the death of a relatively young husband and father. The deceased had collapsed on the sidewalk in the early morning on his way to work. Little could have prepared the officer and his partner for the response of the multi-generations that resided together in the family home. The demonstrative and highly emotional response was unsettling and triggered for one of the two police officers, in particular, a sense of personal vulnerability.

That vulnerability manifested itself in an unusual way. Prior to returning to the police station to end their shift, the officer stopped at his home to hug and hold his sleeping one-year-old son. Impressively, when his supervisor became aware of the event, he recognized the emotional impact the call had had on the young police officer. Going home and hugging a sleeping son in the middle of a call for service is not normal.

The supervisor did a number of things right. The first was creating an environment where that information came to light and was not ignored. Doing something with that information was the second, even if it was simply reaching out to me as the Critical Incident Program Coordinator.

I connected with the two officers at the end of their shift as they were preparing to attend court later that morning (a frequent occurrence for front line police officers). We arranged to meet that morning. By 10:00 a.m. I was sitting with the two officers in a Tim Horton's coffee shop.[3] For two hours, I listened to their story and discussed why events impact us in unique and sometimes unexpected ways. I found myself receiving two great big bear hugs from the uniformed officers, whose physical presence typified the stereotype of the strapping young police officer – all of this taking place in the middle of a busy parking lot. Predicting our responses to critical events is impossible. The desire to hug his son was what unfolded in his recognition that life is precious and unpredictable. And no life was more precious at that moment than the life of his young son. He didn't want to wait until he got home later that day to do what he needed to do and was fortunate to have the luxury to make the necessary detour. I can envision that scene in a Norman Rockwell painting depicting precious moments.

What is amazing about developing genuine, supportive relationships is that you will always know when you get it right. I am so grateful that a caring and insightful supervisor gave me the rich opportunity to connect with two impressive young officers. I was fortunate to be

---

3   I know what you're picturing or at least thinking – three cops sitting in a coffee shop eating donuts. Didn't happen! I have spent most of my career refusing to feed the stereotype.

a part of something that I am sure shaped them both in their role as police officers, but also in their growing and expanding roles as husbands and young fathers.

It is important to recognize the work of the supervisor who created a working environment where he became aware of something very personal happening outside of the office environment. That can only happen when a supervisor focuses on more than just production, performance, and what many organizations call 'the bottom line'. Being willing to spend time getting to know a little about the employees under your influence is fundamental. The supervisor was well aware of the officer's young son and his relatively new responsibilities of being a father. Getting to know those details about an employee doesn't usually take place while sitting behind a desk. It is more in line with the concept of 'leadership by walking around', where executives, managers, and workplace leaders spend significant time interacting with employees on the warehouse floor, production line, or whatever defines your operational workspace. Without that foundation it is difficult, if not impossible, to recognize or hear about the critical events taking place in the lives of your employees.

Notifying a family of a death is a unique responsibility that doesn't usually fall outside the realm of those involved in emergency, medical, palliative, or pastoral care. Other than workplace injuries, of which there are many, most personal crisis moments will occur outside of the workplace. There are, however, indicators in the workplace supervisors could and should recognize. Changes in demeanor or levels of energy, alterations in how talkative someone might be or someone being more withdrawn are all indicators of challenges employees may be facing. In order to recognize a change, it is important for supervisors to establish a baseline. That takes time, energy, commitment, and the ability to pay attention to detail. Getting to know your staff is key, but any supervisor can accomplish that if they make it a priority and are willing to put in the required effort.

Every employee is likely connected to one or two sets of parents or grandparents. It is more likely for children to bury their parents than it is for parents to bury their children; the later usually falling in the category of when REALLY bad things happen. It is also predictable that employees, particularly long-term employees, will face the responsibilities of caring for elderly family members and eventually dealing with the aftermath of their deaths.

My father-in-law, Henry Buller, was an impressive physical specimen at six feet, four inches tall and weighing well into the 200-pound range comprised primarily of muscle. His natural strength made physical labor of any kind seem like child's play. During the summer of 1997, at the age of sixty-one, he was completely surprised with a diagnosis of melanoma.

His prognosis was poor. As a result, he chose to decline prolonged chemotherapy, radiation, or any other aggressive treatments, believing that they would compromise the quality of his remaining life. While I would have loved much more time with my father-in-law, I am thankful for the round of golf he was able to enjoy just weeks before his passing.

When his health started to fail, it deteriorated quickly. He disliked hospitals, and that may have been as much a factor as any in the 'end of life' choices that he made. My wife Sylvia and I welcomed him and my mother-in-law Mary Buller into our home, where arrangements were made to provide palliative care for what would be the last ten days of his life. To this day, I view having them in our home for those ten days to be a privilege.

On October 27th, 1997, he died peacefully in our home surrounded by the people he loved and who loved him. His death, as prepared as we thought we were, unsettled us. Seemingly healthy, physically strong men in their early sixties don't just die.

I was fortunate at the time to work in an amazing environment and under leadership that emphasized team building and strong interpersonal relationships. Staff Sergeant Wayne Bellingham modeled strong and effective leadership that extended outside the documented orga-nizational goals and objectives, touching on the personal realm. Wayne knew the names of the husbands, wives, girlfriends, boyfriends, and partners of every staff member in the unit. He also knew the names of my two children. Wayne had always shown a personal interest in his staff and when the circumstances of my father-in-law arose, he was both attentive and supportive to my needs. Because of the environment that he created, my entire workplace followed his lead. And the support that was extended to myself and my family was not unique. I knew this because I had watched it happen when others in my workplace experienced a crisis. It was simply the standard that had been established for the times when tragedy touched the life of one his staff. It was so much more than approving bereavement leave and the sending of cards and flowers. Not to minimize those acts of kindness, it was the conversations, the interest that he showed in the weeks and months that followed that made his leadership stand out.

I remembered that example of leadership when I assumed my new responsibilities as Wellness Officer. Asking a lot of personal but non-intimate questions became a part of getting to know people and establishing rapport. Paying attention to detail and the little things needed to become second nature. I was uniquely positioned within our organization to respond to bad things happening, but having a title was not something I could rely on if I hoped to make a difference. Credibility and trust are not given indiscriminately; they must be earned, particularly in situations where a person's vulnerability may be exposed. Nothing precludes front line supervisors from doing what that supervisor did for that young father who needed to hug his son or how Wayne responded both during and after the tragic passing of my father-in-law. Supervisors just need the tools, and in some cases the encouragement, to step outside of their comfort zone and start the conversation that gets them involved. When supervisors provide this type of personal care and support they move organizations into the category of 'employers of choice'. Given the diminished loyalty and increased mobility of the current generation of employees, organizations that are recognized as 'employers of choice' are significantly advantaged.

The opportunity to respond to bad things happening is not restricted to those involved in law enforcement or emergency services work nor is it restricted to people with special titles or roles. Opportunities exist for every supervisor and they exist in every workplace. The key is supervisors investing in the lives of those they have been given the responsibilities to lead. Getting to know your staff will create opportunities to know when a staff person is going through a storm. That storm could be a friend or family member battling with cancer or possibly the challenges with caring for an elderly parent who has been diagnosed with Dementia or Alzheimer's disease. Perhaps that storm is the loss of a child during pregnancy or the difficulties parents face raising teenagers in an ever changing and challenging world. Surviving a storm is connected to the lighthouses one sees along the way. As a leader, you can be one of those lighthouses.

Though I grew up as one of five children, my mother had birthed six babies. Peter was the sibling no one ever talked about. I was a teenager when I learned of my stillborn brother, who would have been my parent's third child. What I would learn about Peter, I learned from my siblings. I don't recall either of my parents talking about this loss. While it may have been characteristic of their generation, the silence that followed robbed my parents, and to some extent my two older siblings, the opportunity to openly grieve.

Too many parents have endured this kind of loss in isolation, often denying their pain an avenue for expression. In my lifetime, I have seen parents become more willing to share these kinds of losses whether that loss takes place during pregnancy (miscarriage) or during the birthing process (stillborn). I have seen heartfelt and genuine support and the compassion extended towards these expectant parents. This change is a positive commentary on our society and a reflection of the work in which many in the healthcare industry have engaged. Young families experiencing this type of loss should not retreat to a world of isolation and denial. In addition to connecting on a personal level with your staff they should be reminded that a range of professional and community resources are available.

Leaders have an opportunity in the aftermath of such tragic loss to help shift the way society sees these events, and more importantly, what we do in supporting those whose lives have been impacted.

I was raised by a loving and caring father. After more than thirty years in law enforcement I know that not everyone is so fortunate. What makes my father remarkable to me is that he did not enjoy the experience of a loving and caring father in his own life the way that I experienced in mine.

He was ten years old when on June 30th, 1938, his own father committed suicide by hanging, leaving his wife (my grandmother) to raise their ten children. Fortunately for my grandmother, my father had older siblings including older brothers who stepped into the gap created by an absent father. While I have seen impressive progress in opening up the dialogue in the aftermath of miscarriages and still born deaths, I have not seen the same willingness to process and move past the shame, disgrace, and humiliation that overshadows the grief of family and friends whose lives are forever impacted by suicide. Family and loved ones, including close personal friends who are intimately close to the deceased, are often robbed of the venue to openly grieve.

The first suicide scene I attended as a young recruit in 1987 stands out to this very day, though I would attend many more during my years in the Forensic Services Unit. It stands out because the tragedy involved the hanging of a young man. He had been old enough to have children, which made me think of my father's father. My father never discussed the suicide with me. He never spoke about it, even in the aftermath of the attempted suicide of a young farmer who lived down the road from us. When I attended my first suicide as a recruit, I felt compelled to reach out to my dad. I wrote my dad a letter. It was my way of respecting, at least to some extent, the boundaries he had built up over the course of his life. I was able to acknowledge his loss, recognizing that he never had what I had, and tell him that in the face of such difficult circumstances he was an amazing dad.

While in the process of writing this book, I discovered a letter written by my father in 2005 that he titled "My Story" where he detailed his recollections of that horrific day. He described his story as "a story locked behind clenched teeth for fifty years" sharing it on only three occasions because of consuming emotions, feelings of incredible guilt coupled with an overwhelming sense of shame. In his story my father stated, "Why? Why? Why would my father do this? What had I done to make him choose this?" Such thoughts are common for people paralyzed in the silence that follows such tragic events. My father's story would not have been told had it not been for the counsel of a good friend who stated "Until an emotional wound is acknowledged, it cannot heal."

Several years ago, my father suffered a fall that ultimately resulted in him requiring regular dialysis treatments. While his physical dependencies significantly increased and his mobility has been compromised, the best parts of him, his kindness and his goodness have only been amplified. Growing up I do not recall my father being particularly patient. But in recent years he has become more thankful, more kind, and more generous with words of encouragement. I attribute this in part to his coming to terms with the tragic death of his father. The leadership provided by his friend has had a significant impact on my father's disposition. His story, though not repeated often, is no longer "locked behind clenched teeth". It was the dialogue with a friend that made such a difference, a friend who didn't settle with the silence that had been my father's trademark. He engaged my father in a dialogue that ultimately set my father free of the baggage he had carried all these years. My father will turn ninety years old this year and what a gift it has been to witness the healing of his heart.

For the most part, the act of suicide is a decision made by someone whose mind has become clouded. The act of suicide is covered by the umbrella of mental health. We should extend to the surviving victims of suicide the same support, freedom of expression, and encouragement shown to those who's loved ones die of heart disease or cancer, or who are killed in a motor vehicle collision. All are tragic losses, and much work is required to create a healthy avenue of expression for victims left behind. As outside observers to such heart-breaking loss, we need to overtly extend grace (not judgement) and love (not shame) while providing the surviving victims the same encouragement and support extended to anyone in the grieving process.

Suicide is unfortunately far more common than we would like to acknowledge and so it should not be surprising when it impacts someone in your workplace. Suicide is one of the most difficult tragedies to process because of the baggage it leaves behind for loved ones left holding on to the pieces of a shattered life. Suicide, like no other event, will challenge a leader's capacity to step up and engage. Providing support, understanding, compassion, and grace are powerful responses that will be well received. As leaders, our responsibilities do not include fixing the problem because there isn't anything a leader can do to change the tragic loss whether that be the sudden death of a child, the suicide of a family member, or the passing of an elderly parent. Leaders find ways to extend compassion, creative mechanisms of support, and a safe place for dialogue to whatever extent an employee feels comfortable.

It is important to recognize not all critical incidents end in tragedy. But not ending in tragedy does not negate the need, nor the value, the support of an effective leader can bring to a situation.

I had a unique opportunity to walk alongside a young couple whose first child was born with a hole in his heart. The first few years of their life as new parents were anything but typical. They were filled with numerous medical procedures and constant checkups at the hospital until their son's condition had stabilized. It wasn't all smooth sailing but we celebrated the victories, both small and large, along the way. While our contact is no longer as regular, our friendship continues to this day. They are quick to tell others how meaningful my support was during that very dark period of their lives, but the truth of the matter is, I didn't do anything special. I showed up; I listened to their story; we cried; we laughed; and I didn't need a degree or certificate to do any of it.

Shortly after my appointment as Wellness Officer, I was faced with a set of circumstances that I had not anticipated. An employee of our organization was charged with a series of criminal offences. It had not occurred to me that in my role as Wellness Officer, for a police organization no less, I would encounter an employee facing criminal charges of any kind. This circumstance certainly fits that category of 'bag things happening' regardless of how those circumstances came to be. The employee was immediately suspended but remained a part of the organization. The focus of my role was the well-being of our employees, regardless of their workplace status. Considerable thought went into placing that initial call. While my offer of support and my invitation to connect was turned down, that same offer was presented to others who found themselves facing similar circumstances and the response was very different.

One member in particular, charged with impaired driving, welcomed the support he knew would help him, not only to navigate the judicial process, but more importantly the life-changing decisions he recognized needed to happen, especially with his responsibilities as a single father raising an adolescent daughter. His story is a remarkable story of recovery. He would eventually become a contributor to an evening presentation for recruits and their family members. The segment titled 'Real Stories – Real People' focused on the challenges in surviving a career in emergency services work.

Addictions present in many different forms. While alcohol addiction may be the most prevalent, it no longer corners the market. The impact of addiction is felt in the lives of employees in every workplace. Recognizing addictions seems to becoming a greater and greater challenge. Spending time talking about events and activities that take place outside the workplace is one window into the lives of your staff. While you may not be able to prevent the bad outcomes related to decisions that employees make, recognizing a pattern of self-destruction and presenting the offer of support may be the difference between overcoming an addiction and overcoming a loss of some sort connected to that addiction. The cost of addictions can be measured in terms of organizational loss as well as the obvious personal loss. Organizational loss in the form of diminished productivity, absenteeism, pressures on other employees, increased cost in benefits, and the potential liabilities when actions of an employee are impaired. Personal loss presents in the form of wages, relationships, and current and future employment opportunities, in addition to the quality of life that is eroded by an addiction.

There is so much to be gained when leaders are positioned to recognize the indicators of a person in crisis. Positioning oneself to do so is not as difficult as one might expect.

Celebrating the joys that come along the way for an employee is one of the most effective ways of positioning yourself to hear about and be invited into the challenges that life brings. An effective approach when engaging with employees is to personalize your interactions. "How was your and *Sylvia's* weekend?" would send a different message to me than if someone had simply asked, "How was your weekend?" It is a subtle difference but the conversation is so much more personal. Listening to the details of a vacation is an example of celebrating the good. Asking about the soccer or baseball tournament that took place over the weekend involving employees or their children is another opportunity to connect. You can never go wrong in showing interest in the lives of people's children, particularly if you are able to personalize those interactions. Whether activities involve sports or the arts, in the form of dance or music recitals, any interest will be well received. Engaging with people on this personal level will open doors for future dialogue. Again, I am not suggesting that leaders need to become everyone's best friend. In fact, to do so is counterproductive to the occasional need to engage in difficult conversations when addressing workplace performance and other work-related issues. Appropriate, friendly, and casual interactions regarding non-work-related activities and events is both appropriate and essential to setting the stage for those more personal and vulnerable interactions.

All of these examples celebrate life outside of the workplace and set the stage to hear about the challenges that take place in life as well. And rest assured the challenging events are going to happen.

The questions every leader needs to ask themselves are:
- Will you know about the crisis in their lives?
- Will you recognize it when it happens?
- Will you be invited into the process that follows?

- Will you have the tools to respond in a meaningful and encouraging way?
- Will you have the courage to engage?

The following chapters are intended to equip you so you will have the confidence to answer "Yes" to each of the questions presented above.

CHAPTER THREE –
Everyone Has a Story and Every Story Has its Time

Life happens to us all. We are all subject to circumstances that result from living in nature, which is dynamic and evolving, as well as living with human nature, which is interactive and social. Whether tragic circumstances result from nature or human nature, our mortality is undeniable.

Loss is not, however, restricted only to life and death circumstances. Technology has immeasurably affected the way we receive and digest information. The rapid rise of social media has also altered the way we maintain relationships and share our stories with one another. A positive effect of this is accessibility. It has never been easier to share your story or learn about the stories of others. The other side of that coin is that we are often inundated with the stories of others, to the point where we can become desensitized to their tragedies.

As a leader, your story is extremely significant. The experiences you have had are important because you are who you are because of those experiences. Good or bad, our life experiences shape the people we become. But the real benefit of your experience is what you have learned during your journey through the hard parts. Applying what you have learned from the responses of others that just felt right is far more important than telling your story to someone in crisis.

Too often well-meaning leaders think it is important to qualify themselves, and they do so by relating the circumstances that are part of their story. In that moment of connecting, your story should fade into the background, if it should surface at all. Comparing tragic circumstances or loss seldom has the desired effect. Comparing your story to mine, or my story to yours, minimizes someone's story. I am surprised how often I have heard someone make the comment, 'I know what you are going through' or 'I know how you feel'. While their comment may be intended to place an individual at ease, it can have the opposite effect.

Regardless of how well we think we know someone, we cannot fully understand or appreciate how events fit into the context of their life and the effect those events will have. It would be counterproductive to suggest or assume otherwise. The inference alone could exclude you from providing the very support you wish to give.

A leader's capacity to be effective in supporting others in times of a crisis is not dependent on how many or what kind of tragic circumstances they have encountered themselves. It is dependent on their capacity to develop a skill set largely tied to the competencies of interpersonal abilities, courage, communication, and empathy.

Some of the greatest leaders in our world are the teachers in our elementary and junior high schools. The 'work environment' they create for the impressionable lives of their students can have a lasting impact. The role that teachers have with respect to character development is as valuable as the skills and knowledge they impart to their students. Sometimes life's toughest lessons come early on. Two events that have shaped the person I am today took place before I was twelve years of age and the teacher leaders with whom I would cross paths were outstanding.

October 23rd, 1963 was a typical fall day in the Canadian prairies. The harvest was nearly complete. I couldn't have been happier to be spending time with my grandfather, David Dick. I was four years old at the time. We had just arrived at the local grain elevator with a truck full of freshly harvested wheat and had begun the unloading process.

High concentrations of dust had built up inside the shaft of the grain elevator. When an overheated and faulty motor generated a spark, this dust became like dynamite and ignited, causing a large explosion, a flash fire that consumed the entire structure.

Image used with the permission of The Carillon News
(published October 25th, 1963)

While much of that day is hazy and unclear in my memory, one detail was indelibly imprinted on my mind. I vividly remember running out of the north overhead doors of the elevator. I have no recollection of who I ran to or exactly what happened next. I was rushed to the hospital having sustained third degree burns to my face and hands; the only skin exposed at the time of the explosion due to the fact that I was wearing long pants and a hoodie that protected my skin from the intense flames. Fortunately, there were no casualties. The six of us present in the elevator survived the explosion with varying physical and emotional scars.

The recovery time with my grandfather would set the stage for something special between the two of us, a connection that continued until his passing at the age of ninety-one. My grandfather would be an influencing presence in many decisions during my early adult life. I am overwhelmed with the number of occasions where tragic circumstances form the foundation of relationships characterized by depth and ongoing meaningful interactions. While a shared experience often results in a special bond, so can the helpful, meaningful, and genuine support from a leader equipped to listen and respond to an employee's story, or a teacher equipped to recognize the needs of a child.

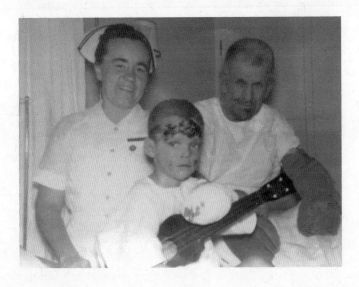

My grandfather and I with our nurse during our recovery in the hospital.

At four, I really didn't recall what life was like before I had scars on both my face and left hand, particularly where skin grafting was required. These scars, for all intents and purposes, have always been a part of who I am. I have seldom been asked about the scars but have never been averse to responding to people who did ask questions. I recall only two specific occasions when my scars became a part of a conversation that had a psychological impact on me.

The first time took place on the school playground and consisted of another boy hurling insults at me, referencing my scars in a way that was clearly intended to be hurtful. The second was during my years at university when, during an application process to become a summer student with the Royal Canadian Mounted Police (RCMP), the recruiter asked me how I would manage should someone target my scars in an effort to provoke me or simply insult or demean me in some way. Fortunately, these types of interactions were the exception. Upon reflection, it is quite remarkable how few of these defining and hurtful moments I experienced.

People, and children in particular, can be very cruel. It would have been totally understandable if my formative years had been riddled with interactions that reminded me of the injuries I sustained at an early age. I looked different - particularly when I started school. I don't dismiss the acceptance I experienced during my early childhood or consider it lightly.

Society's capacity to accept, and in my case, ignore the differences, physical or otherwise, was a reflection of the heart and soul of the people I went to school with. We live in a world where intolerance and isolation is often rooted in fear. Leaders need to do everything possible to influence their workplace towards tolerance, acceptance and inclusion. As leaders we have an obligation, a moral duty, to model that in all our interactions. I am so grateful that the teachers throughout my early years did exactly that.

To support someone you care about who is going through a stormy season, it is critical to understand what to say and when to say it. While I don't recall specific conversations with my teachers at the time, the safe place they created for me assisted in my accepting the scars on my face and hands as there was nothing I could do to change that part of me.

Transitioning from grade school to junior high should be an exciting season of new challenges and opportunities. This is true even if you are a part of a small community where everyone in your grade six class joins you as you enter grade seven. Unfortunately, my first day of junior high was delayed several weeks.

On a blisteringly hot afternoon in late August, I was again injured in a farming accident. I was operating an International TD6 caterpillar, cultivating the ninety-acre field that had just been harvested. The engine was overheating and I had intended to check on it and possibly add water to the levels in the radiator. Unfortunately, the pressure that had built up inside the radiator was so extreme that the safety features of the radiator cap became compromised, sending boiling water twelve feet into the sky and scalding the entire left side of my body.

Despite the intense pain that was immediate, I ran the near half kilometre to our home, leaving the caterpillar running. Fortunately, a nurse friend of my mother was visiting at the time, and knew immediately what to do. She placed me into the shower and began to run cold water over my body to neutralize the burning effect. My mother, who rushed me to the closest hospital thirty-four kilometres away, reached speeds of 150 kilometres per hour. It was extremely fortunate that the flat tire she would experience on her return trip did not occur during our high-speed race to the hospital.

I was fortunate that the burns were not as serious as those I had suffered at age four. The burns to the left side of my body manifested in numerous large blisters, the largest one covering my entire ankle and protruding nearly two inches. I remained in the hospital for several weeks due to the concern of infection, while my body began the rejuvenation process.

My return to school and the normal routine of a twelve-year-old boy was seamless, and again a reflection of the character of my classmates and the kind of environment my teachers and family created.

During the first fifty years of my life I didn't need to tell my story. I am grateful that there was no pressure to talk about my scars nor were any comments made to me about the details of my story. If there were, I was oblivious to them. There are now many more parts to my story and only now are they coming to the surface. But I control the pace, the venue, and the audience. One of the greatest gifts you can extend to someone in crisis it to honor and respect their story, and allow them room to tell it at their pace, in their venue, and for their chosen audience. One of the greatest gifts you will receive in return will be to hear their story.

Everyone has a story and events are taking place all around us. When leaders know how to respond when things go bad so many good things can follow.

CHAPTER FOUR –
Three Responses When Bad Things Happen

Bad things are going to happen in the personal lives of employees in every organization. And every leader will have an opportunity to respond when they do. I have experienced firsthand a range of responses to the critical incidents that took place in my life. I have also witnessed and heard about a similar range of responses from leaders responding to the tragic events in the lives of their staff. The responses could be summarized and placed into the following three categories:

1. People who chose to say or do nothing

You would think that casual acquaintances and strangers would more naturally fall into this category but you would be wrong. Interestingly, those in this group included some close personal friends as well as casual acquaintances.

Certain people I thought would step up during a time of crisis faded into the background. I don't think for a second that there was any malice intended, but truthfully, their lack of demonstrated care hurt. For leaders to say and do nothing is both unacceptable and a missed opportunity. While it may take you well outside your comfort zone, developing the skills to respond to the specifics of your employee's circumstance will add a positive and healthy layer to your relationship and future interactions.

Less than four months after the death of my father-in-law, I developed a large growth on my forehead within a thirty-six-hour period. It was treated as a cyst or unusual infection. I was prescribed antibiotics, and while it initially appeared to respond to them, within weeks it had returned. After several referrals and procedures including a CT scan, I was diagnosed with a brain tumor the size of an egg that had grown through my skull, ultimately presenting as a bump on my forehead.

On June 4th, 1998, the tumor was removed. Following the analysis of the tumor tissue I was diagnosed with an aggressive form of large cell lymphoma. Initially the doctors gave me a two percent chance of survival. I was admitted to the hospital and my treatments began. In the days that followed, and after a series of additional tests, my diagnosis was changed to a very rare and somewhat bizarre presentation of leukemia. This was unusual, in that my blood showed no presence of cancer cells, yet leukemia is referred to as a 'cancer of the blood'. With the change in diagnosis my treatment plan was re-written. The best news was that my chances of survival had gone up considerably. I immediately began my first round of chemotherapy treatments for leukemia followed by a month of site-specific and whole-head radiation treatments.

My life was turned upside down. I was fighting for my life. I was a father of two young children ages five and seven. It was awkward when people didn't respond to the 'elephant in the room'. Tragic events, regardless of the outcome, require a response. You would think that is just common decency and compassion. Failure to, at the very least, acknowledge the tragic circumstance ramps up the volume of silence to deafening heights. As leaders, acknowledging the 'elephant' is just the beginning and can lead to great things.

2. People who responded but missed the mark

I commend the efforts of anyone who steps up during a time of crisis. I assume these efforts are to provide some type of encouragement or support. But, unfortunately, not everyone who does so accomplishes what it is they want to accomplish. I think it is important to recognize that even those who missed the mark with their effort to console likely had the best of intentions. There are a number of reasons for this, but I will focus on two.

Some people have yet to find a place of health and strength following their crisis, and may find it difficult to focus on the needs of others. Someone else's tragic experience is used as a spring board for them to talk about their story. They miss the opportunity to show compassion, support, or encouragement. The focus is on themselves and what can surface is the unresolved pieces of their story.

In my combined thirty-five years working as a police officer and in the social services profession, I have encountered a high number of support workers with a variety of professional titles who have experienced a personal crisis of their own. Many wear their tragic circumstance on their sleeve, having never worked through the pieces of their own story. They have not recognized that recovery is a process that cannot be rushed and that entering into the helping profession is not a recovery strategy. They have yet to find the healthy place they so passionately want to lead others to. It cannot happen until they find the place where they are engaging and supporting others from a place of strength.

The second category of people who tend to miss the mark are people who mean well, but have not made a plan. The adage, 'Failing to plan is planning to fail' has been attributed to the likes of Benjamin Franklin, Winston Churchill, and Alan Lakein, and accurately describes my experiences in the days, weeks, and months that followed my own crisis.

I recall shortly after I celebrated my one-year anniversary being 'cancer free' a conversation with someone whose cousin had also battled cancer. I was told that shortly after celebrating their cousin's one-year anniversary of being cancer free they suddenly relapsed, and had to undergo a new series of treatments. I wonder what went through their mind as they heard the words coming out of their mouth. It was a clear example of missing the mark.

Shared vulnerability is a gift that must be honored and respected. Personal information and the details of someone else's story should never find its way to the water cooler. Surprisingly, it was a 'man of the cloth' who blind-sided us when liberty was taken to publicly talk about our story without our knowledge or permission. People make mistakes and choices are made - we can choose to be hurt and aggrieved or we can choose to extend grace and forgiveness and decide to be unoffendable. To choose anything but the latter hurts us more than anyone. But as a leader avoiding such errors in judgment makes for a rich and very rewarding experience. Treat their story as a gift, and the vulnerability of their character with the respect, honor, and reverence that it deserves.

There are those who have the natural capacity for empathy, care, concern, and support. For them, the right words come easily. For others, empathy and support requires more thought and effort. They may have to prepare for the interactions with people in the midst of a crisis. If you identify with the latter, this book will be a useful tool, and you are well on your way to becoming someone who fits into the third and final group.

3. People whose meaningful response was both timely and appropriate – simply put, it was perfect.

Notice I didn't say profound. I said perfect. As surpris-ing as it was to find close personal friends fade into the background, it was equally surprising to have people who were on the periphery of my life suddenly become welcoming voices of support and encouragement. Interestingly, it was sometimes individuals with little or no personal history with my family and me that made a difference. On some days, the perfect response was simply acknowledging our loss or pain.

Whether your capacity to respond in a heartfelt, meaningful way is a natural part of your DNA, or learned as the result of hard work and preparation, the impact is the same. The good news is that we all have the capacity to become members of this third category.

September 30th, 1998 should have been the day Sylvia and I celebrated our ninth anniversary. We were parents of two young children aged five and seven. But for Sylvia in particular, it was hardly a day of celebration. On that morning, she drove me to the hospital where I was admitted due to complications following my chemotherapy and radiation treatments.

By that time Sylvia was all too familiar with her new routine, which consisted of spending the day at the hospital only to return home in time to meet our children after their day at school. She would then make supper and do all the things that young families do as an evening unwinds.

Little did she know that September 30th would also mark the death of her mother. On October 1st, 1998, two police officers arrived at our home. Despite the fact that I was a police officer, it was immediately apparent that this was not a social call. The officers informed my wife that her mother had been murdered in her home by a stranger, in what appeared to be a senseless act of violence.

Community is shocked, saddened following violent death

by Kristi J Balon

Lac du Bonnet RCMP is investigating the murder of a 63-year-old woman who was found dead in her home October 1.

"The investigation started as the result of Mary Buller being found in her home," said RCMP Cpl. Graham Firlotte.

The corporal said officers from the Lac du Bonnet unit were called to the scene of the crime, five kilometres south of town on Highway 11, at approximately 5:30 p.m.

A friend had become concerned about Buller when she didn't attend a church function. As a result of this concern, the individual went to her home and found her deceased.

"Someone had obviously entered her residence and struck her," said Firlotte. "That was the cause of death."

Mary Buller...
"a very large part of our life"

Image and article used with permission of the Lac du Bonnet Leader
(published October 6th, 1998)4

In the days that followed, while I was in the hospital working on my recovery, Sylvia was meeting with homicide investigators and planning a funeral, all while looking after our two young children.

---

4   Rights to Lac Du Bonnet Leader owned by Clipper Publishing Corp.

Days after the murder, an arrest was made and first degree murder charges were laid against a nineteen-year-old male. While I continued with two more rounds of chemotherapy, the RCMP and the Winnipeg Police jointly continued their investigations. In the summer of 2000, nearly two years after the murder and after weeks of testimony, the evidence would lead a jury to deliver a guilty verdict on the charge of first degree murder. This conviction was later unanimously upheld by three Justices of the Manitoba Court of Appeal.

Any one of the three events that took place in the span of eleven months: the death of my father-in-law, my life-threatening cancer diagnosis, or the murder of my mother-in-law and subsequent trials would have challenged those in our lives in knowing how to respond. But the combination of these horrific and tragic circumstances compounded the difficulties facing those closest to my family and me.

The responses were surprising; some of the surprises were positive and amazing. Unfortunately, that was not always the case. The reality, however, was that Sylvia, and our two young children and I, were not the only ones navigating unchartered waters. It would be completely unfair to be critical of those who may not have gotten it right. We had tremendous support that helped sustain us when we needed it most. We are often reminded of those courageous and steadfast friendships that made such a difference during that very difficult time in our lives.

My workplace was incredibly responsive and while my wife was not connected to an organizational workplace at the time, I wonder what kind of support she would have been offered. I have commented that my job at the time was the easy one as I just needed to focus on my recovery. Even before the murder of Sylvia's mother, her job was much more challenging as she was still primarily focused on my recovery on top of the responsibilities of single parenting two young children while still managing a home. What kind of support would she have experienced as the 'care giver', the healthy one? How well do we respond as leaders when our employees are carrying the added burdens when someone they care about is in crisis?

The husband of one of my staff, who was new to my unit, had become very ill and grew frustrated when attempts to diagnose his condition kept falling short. Working together with her direct supervisor, I thought we had been very supportive. She had been told not to worry about her work and that she should focus exclusively on her care of her husband. She was encouraged to come and go, working as many or as few hours a day as she felt she could manage. I knew I was taking liberties with how sick time benefits could be used but I was prepared to address any issues that could result. Her husband had been rushed to the hospital a number of times and on one occasion he was given the prognosis that he might not recover. It was at that time I knew I needed to step up my support. Going to see her husband in the hospital made the difference. Not in the outcome of her husband's condition, which I am pleased to say has dramatically improved, but in the opinion the member had towards her direct supervisor, myself, and, I think, the organization as a whole. The effort of making a personal connection with her husband had not been foremost in my mind and I regret not taking those steps sooner.

Guidelines for getting it right:
- Avoid asking questions as the starting point

Starting a conversation with a question seldom generates a meaningful dialogue. Introductory questions are seldom open ended and too often simply require a yes/no response.

Questions like "Are you okay?" or "How are you doing?" will predictably generate a response of "Yes" and "Okay", respectively. These responses are even more predictable in interactions with men, especially men in male dominated professions such as police officers, firefighters, or emergency service workers. These professions by their very nature value strength and control. It is not surprising these professions are also guarded with their own sense of vulnerability. Such questions, and others like them, do not encourage people to engage. More often than not, they will shut down communication and leave you with nowhere to go. Trying to revive a dialogue that has been stifled is difficult, if not impossible.

To avoid stifling conversations, think about the potential answers you might get in response to a proposed question. If the potential answers are 'Yes', 'No', or any other one-word response such as 'Fine', Good', or 'Okay', avoid the question entirely.

Leaders predict the need before the 'ask' and then offer support in areas that are appropriate and easily recognizable from an outside observer. Consider the basic necessities of twenty-first century first world living. Using food as an example, we know that everyone needs to eat. In the midst of a crisis even eating takes energy that isn't always available, and preparing what to eat is just not going to happen. Eating healthy would be an even bigger challenge. Consider preparing a meal, organizing a group to do so, or collectively taking advantage of a delivery service, available in most urban centers and have prepared meals delivered to those in need of support. 'I would like to arrange for supper to be delivered to your home on Thursday or Friday' is a very different interaction than 'Is there anything I can do for you?' The only clarification needed after that is to determine if there are any food allergies that need to be considered. This is one of the most basic example of support but nothing precludes people taking creative license in determining their 'offer.' I encourage you to focus beyond our need for sustenance.

Offering to look after specific physical or practical needs gives credibility to your offer of support. Other examples include services such as lawn care or snow clearing. During my extended hospital stay a community group that my wife and I were connected to arranged to have our home cleaned every week.

Help in the form of such tangible and practical gifts was provided to my family during our season of bad things happening. As the recipients of these 'gifts' I can tell you we could never repay their kindness for the support and encouragement their actions provided. What makes such offers so remarkable is that many of these things just happened and to this day we don't know who did what.

But as leaders don't lose sight that creating an opportunity to provide meaningful support can be as much about the giver as it is about the receiver. People often feel helpless not knowing what to do. A leader provides the opportunity for others to become involved, moving them from the category of those who choose to say and do nothing to the category of people who got it right.

- Focus on truth based statements

You can never go wrong with an "I'm so sorry"[5] opening. Don't rush. Let those three words sit there for just a short time. You may be blown away with what silence might generate. Acknowledging the events that have unfolded is the first step in creating a meaningful and supportive dialogue. Acknowledgement is foundational to building rapport with an individual in crisis. Conveying a sense of empathy is a necessary precursor to engaging in dialogue. Genuineness is palpable and sets the tone for everything

---

5   I am a true Canadian and the evidence is in my capacity to apologize to complete strangers for things that really aren't my fault. But in the context of responding to personal crisis the ability to genuinely say, "I'm sorry" is an asset.

else that follows. Genuineness gives way to trust, which must be established before anyone is willing to expose their vulnerability. When you earn the trust of another person and their walls come down, you have truly entered into revered territory.

The next best step is counterintuitive; say nothing at all—practice listening. Give them an opportunity to be quiet and rest in the silence and you may be surprised with the dialogue that follows if you don't hurry to fill the void. Be patient and don't rush the process because there just isn't a quick fix.

If a sense of personal rapport is established, other statements or open-ended questions can then be considered.

Rather than assume you can relate or identify with their situation because of your own journey, I recommend actually stating the opposite. "I can't imagine what you are going through right now" is another truth based statement. We can't know the intricacies of another's life and how relationships are connected or the impact on the tragic events that have unfolded. Assuming that you do can be paralyzing to the relationship.

Now may be another opportunity to say nothing at all—practice listening.[6]

It may be helpful to simply ask, "Are you okay with talking about this?" as a way of seeing if they are ready and interested in a dialogue. Honoring the timing of the telling of their story, the venue, and the audience is

6   Are you sensing a theme?

paramount. This lets them know that you respect their boundaries. If they're not ready or willing to talk, pushing their boundaries too soon may actually prevent them from talking to you when they are ready.

Be prepared for those situations where someone may not be ready to engage at all. I have coached more than a few people on how to respectfully respond to well-intentioned and caring people who actually want to offer genuine support. I have recommended responses of "Thanks for your concern but I'm not at a place where I want to talk about it (whatever it may be)." It's easy to respect those wishes and reinforce your caring with a response that indicates you want nothing but the best for them during the difficult season of their life.

These simple guidelines can assist in setting the stage for you to become a significant support for someone who is hurting.

Do not underestimate the impact of strong leadership in this process. There is no greater mechanism to create a strong sense of team and of purpose than in leading and coordinating a welcomed response to a personal crisis.

My organization is far from perfect. Decisions have been made that impacted my career that I have never understood. But those disappointments have paled in comparison to what people in leadership did for me and my family in the hours of our greatest need. I could never adequately express my gratitude and appreciation for their courage, their personal sacrifice, and the occasional risk they took in doing what they thought was right. It helped me navigate the rough waters of the storms in my life. Be one of those leaders and change the world one interaction at a time.

CHAPTER 5 –
The Paralyzing Misunderstandings of Stress

Chances are you've heard a version of these comments today: "I'm so stressed." "How're you doing?"
(response) "Stressed." There are few issues that receive
more attention than stress. Stress is a daily discussion
point in many workplaces and a frequent talking point in
casual conversations. We seem to carry stress as a badge of
honor for living yet another day.

This constant chatter about stress actually affirms
how little is known or understood about it. Let's start by
giving some meaning to the language of stress. Stress is,
in fact, a neutral term. There are few words in the English
language that can correctly reference both good and
bad, positive and negative, productive and unproductive.
Unfortunately, in our everyday vernacular, stress is often
equated with only one side of the pendulum - the bad,

negative, and unproductive. I am a firm believer that lives would change if we eliminated the word stress from our vocabulary and forced people to use the more descriptive terms of eustress and distress.

Eustress (think: positive stress) is good, positive, and productive and is always present in people who are able to achieve their goals. It is one of the markers of success. There are few motivators greater than eustress, which can create a sense of feeling challenged, productive, and satisfied. Eustress can only be experienced when people extend themselves beyond their comfort zone by pushing the limits of their ability. Everyone benefits from a little eustress in their lives because ultimately it leads to growth. With respect to personal achievement, there is increased potential for really great to happens when we extend beyond our comfort zone. Experiencing eustress helps us to develop new skills, extend our personal boundaries, and accomplish things we may have previously thought impossible.

Distress (think: negative stress), on the other hand, is bad, negative, and counter-productive. People who are distressed are easily paralyzed. They can become stagnant, or even worse, regress in the area of their distress. Unfortunately, distress is like cancer – when it infiltrates one area of life, it will often bleed into other areas of life. Experience enough distress in your life, and you will begin to feel your life spinning out of control.

Control is key in understanding our capacity to foster eustress and minimize distress in our lives. Before we are able to establish a level of control in our lives we need to recognize that simply saying we are 'stressed' does nothing to help us take control or move forward. Today, saying that you are 'stressed' is a common excuse for mediocrity and more often than not we allow people to get away with it. We often don't ask questions, challenge one another, or direct the conversation towards strategies for healthy living.

Distress is a state of mind that manifests itself in many different ways. When someone says that they are stressed, they are really saying that their life is being affected by a distress that is negatively impacting the quality of their life. Improving their quality of life will require more than just talking about how stressed they are. Being stressed is not a badge of honor that reflects how hard someone works, nor is it a reflection of the importance of one's responsibilities. Rather, being in a constant state of distress reflects the inability to deal with circumstances of one's life. This inability to cope may stem from a lack of experience, training, maturity, support, or understanding.

Distress is inevitable and can be a significant motivator to make positive changes in one's life. Positive changes are more likely when people's intention and focus is matched by their dedication and perseverance.

Leaders can challenge the current mindset by listening to the statements of employees and can encourage an evaluation of what is on their plate or an evaluation of the focus of their energy. Is the energy they are expending moving them towards a less distressing state? If you suspect not, initiate one of those difficult conversations followed by encouragement and support.

Eustress is what leaders experience as they step outside of their comfort zones and engage with an employee following a personal crisis. Distress is what they will experience should they be ill prepared for that interaction and it does not go well. Knowledge and experience in the process will equip leaders to engage with an employee and present an offer of support and know how to respond even when the offer of support is not accepted.

CHAPTER 6 –
Common Signs and
Symptoms of Distress

Trauma is not to be confused with a critical event or tragic circumstance. Critical events can result in a variety of distress reactions, and distress reactions can lead to trauma. The good news is that not all distress reactions necessarily lead to trauma; in fact, very few do. To say that someone has experienced something traumatic is assuming a loss before the race has even begun. The burns I sustained as a child or the horrific murder of my mother-in-law could have been traumatic, but they weren't. Being traumatized and being impacted/forever changed are not one and the same. Being traumatized relates to intensifying and prolonged distress reactions. Being impacted/forever changed can manifest in countless positive ways.

There are many common signs and symptoms of distress that are normal and healthy responses of the mind and body when exposed to events that fall outside the everyday realm of human experience. These distress reactions are normal responses of normal people who are experiencing something that is not normal.

Common signs and symptoms of distress reactions that I have observed or heard described and that are well documented can be categorized into one of four categories:

1. <u>Physiological distress reactions</u> include chest pain, chills, difficulty breathing, dizziness, elevated blood pressure, fainting, fatigue, grinding of teeth, headaches, muscle tremors, nausea, profuse sweating, rapid heart rate, thirst, twitches, vomiting, visual difficulties, and weakness.

Physiological distress reactions are most often experienced in the immediate aftermath of a critical event. They usually dissipate quickly following the reestablishment of order and calm. Critical events happening outside the workplace will make observing these particular distress reactions difficult. However, physiological distress reactions may be described by an employee who is telling his or her story and therefore it is important to understand how they fit into the overall experience. It is also not uncommon that the telling of their story triggers the very same physiological distress reactions experienced at the time of the crisis.

2. <u>Cognitive distress reactions</u> include assigning blame, confusion, decreased attention span, heightened or lowered alertness, hyper-vigilance, increased or decreased awareness of surrounding, intrusive images, memory disorientation of time, nightmares, poor abstract thinking, poor concentration, poor decision making, poor problem solving, suspicion, and uncertainty.

One of the cognitive distress reactions is that memory is impacted. Victims of a critical event will sometimes experience gaps in their recollections or issues with recalling the sequence of events. It is like a puzzle where some pieces don't seem to initially fit, while other pieces are outright missing. Time is our best friend with respect to this cognitive symptom, however, in the cases of extreme distress, memories may never be fully restored. It has been more than fifty years since I ran out of that grain elevator and I am still missing significant pieces of that day from my memory. I have accepted that they are likely to remain missing.

Cognitive distress reactions may be observed in the workplace of someone who has experienced a storm in his or her personal life. Poor concentration and or seemingly a lack of being present are common cognitive distress reactions that linger, sometimes well after individuals have reengaged with their regular routines. In certain workplaces, these lapses in focus can become a safety risk. Someone who is physically present in the meeting room or the lunchroom but who is totally unengaged or lost in his or her own thoughts may reflect consuming and overwhelming thoughts connected to a personal crisis.

3. <u>Emotional distress reactions</u> include agitation, anger, apprehension, anxiety, denial, depression, emotional outbursts, fear, feeling overwhelmed, grief, guilt, inappropriate emotional response, intense irritability, loss of emotional control, and panic.

Emotional distress reactions are usually recognized when responses and interactions with co-workers and/ or supervisors are out of character. Outbursts of anger from someone who is usually very composed, or intense irritability from someone who is normally exceptionally tolerant, would be flags that a conversation is warranted.

4. <u>Behavioral distress reactions</u> include antisocial acts, change in social activity, change in speech patterns, change in usual communication patterns, erratic movements, hyper-alertness to environment, inability to rest, increased alcohol consumption, intensified pacing, loss or increase of appetite, and withdrawal.

Any change in behavior suggests something is going on. Increased alcohol consumption or other forms of addictive habits require a leader to engage in a purposeful conversation.

Any one of the distress reactions listed above are normal responses of normal people in the aftermath of an event that is anything but normal. We will know that we are processing the impact of a critical event well when the frequency of the distress reaction and the intensity of the distress reaction reduces over time. This signifies that the symptoms of distress are being managed well. If the symptoms of distress remain constant or increase in frequency and intensity over time, additional and professionally trained support may be necessary.

One of the greatest barriers to a timely and full recovery is fear. Fear of what someone is experiencing. When leaders pay attention and initiate meaningful and purposeful conversations, recovery from the distress reactions stemming from a critical event can help accelerate the recovery process.

These normal human reactions fall into one of three diagnostic categories:

1. *Critical Incidents (CI) – Symptoms lasting forty-eight hours or less;*
2. *Acute Stress Disorder (ASD) – Symptoms lasting thirty days or less;*
3. *Post-Traumatic Stress Disorder (PTSD) – CI symptoms lasting longer than thirty days and causing reduction in normal functioning.*

The symptoms of PTSD are no different than those symptoms that follow anyone who has experienced a critical incident. The key to preventing PTSD is early intervention and support. What does early intervention and support look life for the average workplace, those workplaces outside of the emergency services industry?

Without minimizing the value of what I did as Wellness Officer or inflating the role I had in the healthy outcomes of the employees I met with, what I did others can do. For someone who has experienced something outside of their 'normal,' support may simply be the presence of someone in his or her life who possesses the courage, understanding, and wisdom to 'get it right' (referenced in Chapter Three) and responding in a way that invites dialogue. That is what a great leader will do. In his own way, that is what Wayne Bellingham did both in his personal interactions with me and in the leadership he provided in my workplace and the resulting support of my colleagues.

The primary purpose of my role as Critical Incident Program Coordinator with the Winnipeg Police Service was threefold:

1. Provide information about distress, distress reactions, and survival techniques (information that is included in this guidebook);

2. Accelerate the normal recovery processes in normal people who may experience normal distress reactions to totally abnormal events. (While time is our best friend in recovering from the distress reactions that follow a critical event, we can accelerate the process by engaging with our staff and providing a safe and welcoming platform to participate in a dialogue that includes their being able to tell their story.);

3. Provide appropriate resources and support for employees and their families (requires doing the

homework for what is available in your community in addition to what is available through your organization).

As Wellness Officer, I was privileged to connect with people experiencing the aftermath of an event outside their normal experience. However, it does not take a formal position such as Wellness Officer or Critical Incident Program Coordinator to be a support to people in these circumstances. Any leader or friend has the capacity to make a difference. While presented as a guidebook, the material in this book will not make you a mental health care professional, nor will it equip you to engage in therapeutic counselling. It will, however, equip you to initiate a dialogue and position you to make a difference; something that doing nothing will not. Engaging people is a productive first step. The necessary step that follows is putting in place a plan for healthy recovery.

CHAPTER 7 –
Why Me? The God Question
(Unpacking the Spiritual Dimension)

Resources that focus on trauma don't often include a spiritual component. Yet for those who have such a framework, I believe this topic warrants attention, whether that spirituality is an active part of an individual's life or not. It is important to at least scratch the surface on the issue as many individuals in the workplace may find themselves wrestling with their spiritual identify during a life crisis.

I recognize the diversity of spiritual experiences and that the language used to describe spirituality varies from one faith group to another. Some refer to spirituality as belief in a greater power or a force that exists outside of our physical presence. To be as inclusive as possible I will use 'God' as the focus and centre of our discussion of spirituality. I hope that anyone who uses different terms and language will be able to make the necessary adjustments.

Questions like "Why me?" or statements like "Life isn't fair." are commonly heard in the aftermath of tragedy. Failing to process these questions or thoughts adequately can be as damaging as failing to work through more commonly recognized distress reactions.

The 'Why Me? The God Question' identifies how spirituality is tied to tragedy and the distress reactions that result.

How individuals link their experiences with their own spirituality, including their understanding of God, may be directly connected to each of the four distress reactions previously discussed.

For those with a spiritual framework, failing to effectively process events from a spiritual perspective can result in intensified cognitive and emotional distress reactions. This can also impact how connected they are to their social support network.

Death and other critically distressing events often leave people feeling very alienated, questioning their spiritual framework to the point where they abandon aspects of their life that had been foundational to who they are.

Cognitive distress reactions can surface in the form of doubt, or questions like, Is there a God? Is God in control? Why would God cause bad things to happen? Am I being punished for past indiscretions? Is this a part of God's plan for my life? This type of spiritual questioning can result in confusion, blame, uncertainty, and poor decision making, which are all cognitive distress reactions.

The God question is often connected to emotional distress reactions, such as developing a bitterness or even hatred for God, the church, and anyone connected to that part of one's life. Feelings of what I call misplaced guilt or shame for living out a less than perfect life are common. Intense anger and resentment are emotional distress reactions that often follow the questioning of a spiritual framework that may have worked in the past but no longer makes sense in light of the circumstances that have unfolded.

Not resolving the God questions may result in behavioral distress reactions such as distancing or isolating themselves from all faith related contacts or activities. This withdrawal creates an isolation from what may have been integral supports. This may in turn delay the recovery process.

Depending on the intensity of any related cognitive, emotional, or behavioral distress reactions, the possibility exists for heightened physiological distress reactions as well. While physiological distress reactions are most often experienced in the immediate aftermath of a critical event, they may also surface when other distress reactions increase in frequency or intensity over time.

Regardless of what a person's spiritual journey has been, I cannot overstate the value of doing the hard work to reconcile the questions a tragedy may create. Those nagging spiritual questions can do more harm than most people recognize.

It would be impossible for me to present a prescriptive process, as the spiritual journey is as unique as the individuals themselves. But I can state with tremendous confidence from personal experience that reconciling one's life experience within a spiritual framework will accelerate recovery and a return to everyday life.

My hope is that anyone who has been impacted by a tragic event finds their way to a place of peace and rest. Being at peace and rest is a great place to be in the aftermath of when things go bad. As leaders, you have an opportunity to encourage anyone going through a storm in their life to work out their spiritual questions, whatever they may be. Leaders don't need to share the same spiritual framework to provide the support that is often needed for individuals to undertake the work required. Leaders don't need a Religious Studies degree, as those with a spiritual framework will likely know the resources that relate to their background. A degree isn't required to ask the right questions and to then provide encouragement in their pursuit for wholeness.

Wholeness will only be realized when the impact of a personal crisis can be reconciled at every level, including the spiritual dimension.

My story would not be complete without the inclusion of how I wrestled with this very issue. It is, however, not my intention to proselytize to anyone and that is why I have included my spiritual journey through the aftermath of bad things happening as an appendix. I hope that by including the process of reconciling my life experience with my personal spiritual framework as an appendix, this part of my story can be appreciated by those interested and easily set aside by those who are not.

CHAPTER 8 –
You're Not Crazy:
Healthy Responses to Crisis

As we've discussed, distress reactions are normal responses of normal people who have experienced something that is not normal. Many of these normal responses are initially involuntary and occur when our senses are overloaded with stimuli. Some of the responses may be linked to a predisposition of the mind and body.

That being said, distress reactions are not random. This is why it is so important to form habits that encourage eustress responses instead of distress reactions. That is not to say that we should embrace and find enjoyment in every life circumstance. That is not possible. But developing a eustress response enables us to move towards a life that is marked by productivity, success, growth, control, and resilience.

In the hours and days that follow a horrific event it would be normal to want to take time to stop, breath, and settle yourself. While this is normal, it is critical not to get stuck here. Knowledge is power and being informed is key to not only surviving an event, but thriving in the aftermath. Being informed about distress reactions (those that potentially lead to PTSD), and their impact, prevents individuals from thinking they are going crazy. Providing information about our responses in the midst of a crisis, and normalizing the symptoms someone may be experiencing, can be liberating and accelerate the recovery process.

During the seven years I spent as Critical Incident Program Coordinator for the Winnipeg Police Service, I had occasion to meet with hundreds of members and their families relating to numerous critical events that fit into one of the following three categories:

1. Threat to life encounter

An obvious example is incidents where an officer's life was threatened by a suspect with a deadly weapon. I observed that in these circumstances, whether or not the incident resulted in injury or death did not determine the resulting distress reaction or lack thereof.

Threat to life encounters are more commonplace than what I have described for those involved in the policing profession. Other examples include being involved in a serious motor vehicle collision, being given a life threatening medical diagnosis, and surviving one of nature's storms (hurricane, tornado, fire, flood). Certainly, my experience as a four-year-old fits into the category of threat to life encounter. The distress reactions that can follow any one of these events need to be given the same attention as any physical injury that requires some type of treatment or care. When critical incidents are processed well, great things can come out of a tragic circumstance. The shared experience with my grandfather David Dick created a deep bond between us, one that would continue until his death at the age of ninety-one. I loved my grandpa and was always looking for ways to introduce him to new experiences. At the age of eighty-four I was able to take him ice skating for the first time. A few years later I was also able to convince him to join me for an exhilarating motorcycle ride on my Honda Gold Wing 1200.

Similar to physical injuries, some will heal on their own while others require the assistance of professionals. Effective leaders should know what resources are available within their organization. What kind of support and allowances can be made based on negotiated benefits? What will the top executives support? It is not uncommon in light of exceptional circumstances for support to be offered that exceeds what is articulated in the collective bargaining agreement.

At the time of my illness I was working in the Forensic Identification Unit under the leadership of Staff Sergeant Wayne Bellingham as I have previously mentioned. Wayne's leadership was progressive both in the technical work of forensic science and in his attentiveness to the needs of the people who worked under his command. He was constantly thinking outside the box. It was no wonder the Winnipeg Police Service was the first agency in Canada to acquire an Automated Fingerprint Identification System. Wayne was never one to sit back and wait for someone else to chart the way. Looking after his staff was no different. He was a risk taker and sometimes that just meant doing what he thought was right. During my initial course of chemotherapy, which lasted six weeks, I was placed in an insolation ward in Winnipeg's largest hospital. Access was both restricted and closely monitored to prevent the patients from infections given that their immune systems were compromised. Sylvia visited me every day and there was not one occasion when she needed to worry about transportation or parking. Daily rides to and from the hospital were simply a phone call away. My colleagues doubled as Sylvia's chauffeur every time she needed a ride. Besides the obvious benefit of not needing to drive and park, the regular contact with people who had been a big part of my life was valued by both Sylvia and my colleagues who were just glad to be able to do something that was meaningful. Those opportunities took place because of the leadership that Wayne provided. He taught us all what being a part of a healthy and supportive work family could look like. Sadly, on December 14th, 1999, Wayne passed way after his own battle with cancer, having been diagnosed with melanoma earlier that year. The gift he had given us in modeling what it looked like to care for each other remained with us. And at the time of his passing we needed it more than ever.

Never underestimate the value of creativity. The liberties that Wayne took and the practical support that was provided may not be possible in your work environment. There is no script for what support can look like. Just don't settle for doing nothing. Brainstorming, if necessary, should involve those willing to offer support, not those whose lives have been turned upside down. You can't go wrong if it fits into the categories of kindness and generosity, the two words that I would use to describe Wayne.

2. Exposure to death

Responding to the suicide of a seven-year-old is an event that most police officers will thankfully never experience. Multiple or violent death scenes fall into their own category, and their impact on police officers is as diverse as the situations themselves. Investigating a triple homicide or a fatal fire resulting in five deaths leaves lasting images that can require considerable and intentional efforts to reach a place where the distress reactions are manageable.

People working outside of the emergency services or medical professions may not normally encounter death as part of their normal work environment. That does not mean others are insulated from such an experience. An unexpected exposure to death may result in a host of distress reactions. These distress reactions are often felt on a very personal level. Understanding that these distress reactions are healthy and normal can be very significant in the healing process.

Providing palliative care for an elderly parent will predictably expose family members to a personalized experience with death. But death can be random. I recall visiting a former colleague in the hospital. I knew he wasn't doing well but was not expecting to find myself at his bedside when he breathed his last breath. His family members had stepped out for a few minutes to eat a late lunch. None of us have the answers to all life and death questions, but it would not surprise me if death in this instance had been in some way chosen by my colleague to protect his loved ones. While I just happened to be present, it could have been anyone in that hospital room.

3. Event is personalized in some manner (often including the overlapping of professional and personal lives, particularly for those involved in the medical field or emergency services)

It was surprising to see how often events unfolded where the professional lives of police members intersected with their personal lives. The most notable example of this during my years as Wellness Office occurred one night when a young police officer answered the call from a dispatcher. As requested, he attended to the local Trauma Center, where a female victim of a motor vehicle collision had been transported. Shortly after his arrival, the attending physician acknowledged that they had done all they could, but that the woman had not survived her injuries.

The medical staff turned over the deceased's purse, containing the women's identification. It was only then that the member realized the deceased was the wife of his best friend. He had been in their home the previous night and had enjoyed a dinner together. While informing his best friend of the death of his wife was likely the most difficult task of his career, the officer wanted no one else to assume that responsibility.

In the conversations that followed over the years I know that the police member pulled out all the bright colored threads of what was a very black and dark day. He would eventually become another contributor in the training for new members and their families called 'Real Stories – Real People', which became a way of honoring the memory of his best friend's wife and part of his own healing.

Death happens every day. It is surprising how often it happens in the lives of those around us. The family of a colleague of mine experienced two such tragedies:

- The sudden and unexpected life-threatening injury of a healthy grandmother; and
- The sudden and horrific death of a six-month old baby girl who had been suffering from what appeared to be a common virus or flu.

So, what is the appropriate response in these circumstances? Is there anything that can be said or done that can make it easier? So often people think there is nothing they can do that will make a difference, so they drift silently into the background. My hope is that you will immediately consider the three responses described in Chapter 3, and engage. Engage in such a way that invites dialogue, recognizing that now is a perfect time to listen to their story. That's what I had the privilege of doing with my colleague, hearing about the family that had been devastated and how each of them was connected to my colleague. What a privilege it was to hear his story.

Personalized events occur in ways outside of those relationships where there is a direct connection between victims and those engaged in the aftermath. I recall early in my years as a Forensic Crime Scene investigator attending to the brutal beating of a five-year-old girl by her father that had left her in a life-threatening condition. I recall entering the crime scene, which could have been a home in my neighborhood, and noting in particular a drawing that had been attached to the fridge. It was clearly the proud drawing of the young girl. The drawing stood out for me as they replicated similar drawings that my daughter, five at the time, had brought home following a day at kindergarten. As a scene photographer, I would later be assigned to attend the hospital and photograph her injuries and the procedure during which her heart valves were harvested. She died shortly thereafter. We don't often get to choose our work, and it was one of my peers who stepped up when it came to attending the autopsy (a requirement in all violent death investigations) and flat out told me that he would be attending the autopsy despite it being my responsibility. He knew I had a daughter the same age and didn't want me adding any more images into my mind than I had already been exposed to. It wouldn't surprise me if he did so under his own initiative or if any one of the supervisors in our unit had suggested it. They were all of the same mindset; we take care of our own. That was the tone, the expectation, and the example of our leader at the time. Examples in your workplace are likely to look very different but the message leaders need to communicate is the same; we take care of our own.

Depending on your role or position, and the relationship you have with those facing life-changing, difficult, and critical circumstances, the information on distress reactions may be helpful as they process the aftermath of their version of 'when things go bad'.

People who find themselves in these unchartered waters need to know just how normal they are, and that they are not crazy. Recognizing that what they are experiencing is normal and healthy can be impacting on their recovery process. A healthy recovery sets the stage to embrace and celebrate whatever the future brings.

Let me recount another experience that I have witnessed and am confident takes place in many work environments, regardless of the industry or type of organization.

You may be familiar with the definition of insanity being someone doing the same thing over and over and expecting different results. That thought has crossed my mind when confronted with that person who is always in crisis or a state of distress, continuously reporting on how difficult their life is. It is like they have made a conscious decision that being a lifelong victim works for them. Every workplace has that person people avoid asking: "Hi, how are you?" because the answer is the same every time, a long monologue of how difficult and unfair life is. Here is a tactic that I have found works, or at least it has reduced the occasions where I hear the same response. When speaking with such an individual, ask questions that reorient the conversation to a focus on his or her choices.

- What steps are you taking to make sure that
  (… Insert Challenge …)
    - doesn't continue?
    - starts to get better?
    - situation changes?
- You mentioned that the last time we talked and it doesn't seem like much has changed. Have you considered seeking professional help?
- Have you found any good resources that would help you deal with (… Insert Challenge …)? There is so much out there.

Interrupting their cycle of rehearsed victimization by orientating them towards change, solutions, and taking control of their circumstances is the greatest gift you could offer them.

Listening to their well-rehearsed autobiography of pain and suffering will not be useful to them and is not a particularly good use of your time and energy.

CHAPTER 9 –
The Lie Everyone
Wants You to Believe

One of the biggest misunderstandings of tragedy, turmoil, or really difficult experiences, is the concept of 'closure.' Many believe that at some point in time, or as the result of some specific event, those living out the aftermath of a critically distressing event will experience closure.

This misunderstanding needs to be dispelled immediately because it's a lie - closure doesn't happen. And quite frankly, I don't want it to. You don't simply put a tragic experience behind you or move on. Tragic circumstances change you. You don't suddenly recover from them, any more than you can wave a magic wand and pretend the 'bad thing' didn't happen. That is not to say that you stay stuck in the tragedy. That would result in becoming a lifelong victim, and there is way too much life to live to allow that to happen to yourself or someone you care about.

Tragic circumstances shape you in ways that nothing else can. From my own experience, I am a different person because of the scars that have marked my physical appearance since I was just four years old, and again at the age of twelve. I didn't experience closure when I was released from the hospital, or when my scars finally healed from the burns that would mark my appearance. I have developed a greater sensitivity and tenderness for those who carry physical characteristics that make them stand out in a crowd.

I am a completely different person because of my experience walking alongside my father-in-law as he lived out his last days in our home. I didn't find closure when the body of Henry Buller was laid to rest following a graveside ceremony. I have had to process, and continue to wrestle with and respect the choices that he made with respect to the aggressive treatments he declined. I have had to learn how to respect the choices that others make. I continue to learn how to walk alongside people who may make different choices from the ones I would make if faced with similar circumstances.

I am a completely different person because of the threat to life I, as a husband and young father of two children, experienced when a diagnosis of cancer turned my world upside down. I am a completely different person because of the diagnosis, surgeries, and subsequent chemotherapy and radiation treatments I underwent. While the outcome of my treatments continues to be more than I could have asked, hoped, or imagined, the desired results did not bring resolute closure. I didn't find closure when my treatments ended or when I was discharged from the hospital; nor did I experience closure when I celebrated my ten-year anniversary of being cancer free. My healing has become a frequent trigger for a spirit of thankfulness, a sense of both joy and peace and a reminder of what's really important. This medical crisis brought people and resources into my life that changed every part of me. Those changes have been profound, particularly in the spiritual arena.

I am a completely different person because of the experience of losing my mother-in-law as the result of a homicide. Closure didn't happen when an arrest was made; nor did it happen when the jury reached a guilty verdict or when the Court of Appeal upheld the findings of the jury. The circumstances of the tragic and horrific loss of my mother-in-law and all the aftermath is a thread in the tapestry of my life that cannot be removed, archived, or denied. Reminders of her absence from our lives appear both predictably on certain dates or at certain events, but also at times arrive unannounced when least expected.

One date in particular has become for me a representation of 'it was the best of times – it was the worst of times.'

- September 30th marks both the celebration of my marriage to my life partner, Sylvia Buller Isaak

(1989) and the horrific and tragic murder of my
mother-in-law Mary Buller (1998).

I draw attention to this date to highlight the reality that
life doesn't unfold in a neat and orderly fashion. Life is
messy and we find ourselves living in a world where joy
and sorrow are often inseparable. Memories often arrive
without warning, memories that can be momentarily
paralyzing. They can drop us to our knees both figura-
tively and literally. While I can prepare for an anniversary, I cannot prepare for the sight of an elderly couple
holding hands while walking down the sidewalk on a
beautiful summer night. This was a real-life circumstance
that created for me an image of my in-laws Henry and
Mary Buller; lives cut much too short; reminders of birth-
days and Christmas celebrations they were never able
to experience.

While those moments are hard, they are also rich. That
is a decision I make; mourn their loss but also celebrate
the gift of having known them and the privilege of having
been part of their family. That is my challenge. It is one
that continues to this very day. And each time it happens
I am reminded that I continue to make choices every day;
choices that ultimately determine the legacy of my life.

In the immediate aftermath of the murder of Mary
Buller, Sylvia became detailed orientated. Her focus was
on the many tasks at hand, including my care and being
a single parent of two school age children. Rides to the
hospital, preparation of a meal, offers to do the laundry,

vacuum and clean the house, and cut the grass were more welcomed by her than conversations about the difficulties surrounding her.

Sylvia had been denied the opportunity to properly grieve the death of her father by my diagnosis with cancer. Grieving the murder of her mother was then put on hold while my medical condition demanded her time, energy, and focus. But grief delayed is not grief denied.

Grieving continues to this present day in wonderful ways. I am so proud of Sylvia and our children who continue to honor Henry and Mary Buller in their own ways. The legacy of Henry and Mary Buller lives on in the lives of their daughter and grandchildren.

At the time of their grandma's death our daughter Jessica was seven and a half years old, and our son Hudson was about to turn six. Our children provided us a very rich and real experience as they processed their own loss. The impact of loss in the lives of our children is unique - different from that of an adult. To witness their raw emotion and uninhibited candor was precious and something we value to this day. Their grief and healing continues as much as it does for Sylvia and myself. At the age of twenty-two, our son Hudson had a tattoo created to honor his grandmother. The tattoo is placed on the inside of his left bicep next to his heart, and depicts a hummingbird and a petunia (his grandmother's favorite bird and flower) with a reproduction of her actual signature (Mary) as a lower banner.

Honoring the life of someone we love will always be a personalized response and does not follow a schedule. I am so proud of how Hudson has chosen to represent the relationship he had with his grandmother.

How you choose to honor or mark a particular event in your life will be different than how anyone else would mark the same event. There is no script or schedule that is predetermined. What you do and when you do it are secondary. The important thing is to honor someone or mark an event in a way that is authentic, genuine, and sincere.

Most of these events took place between ten and twenty years ago, and some more than fifty years ago. To date, I still wouldn't use the word 'closure' to describe my experience or feelings with respect to any one of them. Each of those events has shaped the person I am today and will continue to do so. They have shaped my interests, the things that catch my eye, the choices I have made as I continued my professional development and obviously the things in which I invest my time and resources.

Life happens, and we all have choices to make. It is our choices that will keep us from getting stuck. It is our choices that prevent us from becoming defined by what has happened to us. It is our choices that determine the characteristics that others will use to describe us. It is our choices that define our legacy. Our ability to continue to make good choices in the days, months, and decades that follow tragic circumstances is what enables us to heal and embrace our future, more than any unattainable standard of 'closure' ever could.

Leaders need to recognize this lifelong process and measure their response and the language that they use in their interactions with the survivors of the varied bad things that occur in the lives of their staff.

Regarding Chapter 10 and Chapter 11

Most of what has been presented so far has been presented to those with leadership responsibilities. As mentioned at the outset, the skills needed to effectively lead in a time of personal crisis are different than the skills needed to lead during a time of an organizational crisis. For some leaders, incorporating these skills into the leadership skills toolbox will be natural and almost seamless. For others, it will push them to what feels like the edge of their capacity.

You will recognize that the last two chapters are presented directly to an individual in the midst of a storm, an individual who is navigating through the bad thing that has occurred in his or her life.

Depending on your comfort level to communicate the information presented in these two chapters I have written the material in such a way that you have the ability to simply offer these two chapters to them as a personal resource. As a Wellness Officer and after considerable training and experience, I was comfortable talking about the strategies to reestablish control and for not only surviving the storm, but thriving in its aftermath. With the material presented as it is you have options. If you have risen to the challenge of getting it right and your offer to engage has been well received, don't stop until wounded and hurting people have a plan to establish control of their lives so that they can embrace the new person that they are becoming.

CHAPTER 10 –
Taking Control of Your Life

Taking control of your life is not nearly as complicated as many would have you believe. But it would be a mistake to assume that because the concept is simple the process is easy.

The premise of taking control of your life is that you actually have the capacity to take control of your life. But in order to take control, you have to first accept that it is possible.

So how do you take control of your life?

- Focus on the present with a view toward the future:
    - I have never been one to spend a lot of time and energy analyzing the past. I found little value in beating myself up for something I thought I did that led or contributed to my circumstances. That is not to say we don't learn from our past. I have found that focusing on

the present situation, whatever situation that may be, was much more productive. You will take a significant step through 'your storm' when you can articulate what you want your future to look like.

- Strategies to overcome distress reactions:
  - We have the greatest amount of control over the impact of our <u>behavioral distress reactions</u>, but exercising that control requires discipline. In order to minimize behavioral distress reactions, focus on doing the things that have been a part of your normal routine that bring a sense of security and enjoyment. Additionally, engaging in some form of physical movement such as going for a walk or a bicycle ride will also be helpful, even if it is not normally a part of your day.
  - <u>Cognitive distress reactions</u> can be paralyzing, but it is possible to interrupt thoughts that are fear based. Each time a fear based thought (one that is often associated with a disturbing intrusive image) comes to mind, intentionally turn your thought to something positive - a recollection of a happier time, and continue to focus on the positive memories of your past.
  - Initially, <u>physiological distress reactions</u> are instinctive; an involuntary bodily response to the event unfolding before us. The healthy

and normal evolution of physiological distress reactions is that they should diminish in frequency and intensity over time (like all other distress reactions). Physiological distress reactions are often linked to cognitive distress reactions (which we have greater opportunities to influence - reorienting our thoughts) and can be mitigated by engaging in physical activities that require whole-body movement (a behavioral distress reducing strategy).

- Emotional distress reactions, like physiological distress reactions, are initially instinctive responses to the events unfolding before us. Likewise, the same efforts to reorient our thoughts and engage in physical whole-body movement should be considered. It is difficult for the human body to experience high levels of emotional distress when engaged in physical activity, especially activity that requires an elevated heart rate.

Just as the different kinds of distress reactions are interconnected, so are the strategies to overcome them. To start the recovery process, I recommend the following:

- Focus on behavior. (This is an indirect strategy to shape one's thoughts, with an understanding and confidence that our physiology and feelings will follow the benefits of physical activity).

- Start with a behavioral based plan that is achievable (realistic in scope/scale and short in duration).
- Avoid criticizing, blaming, and/or complaining about behavior or treatment by someone else.
- Celebrate every success, big or small.
- Never give up.
- Adjust scope/scale if necessary.
- Repeat process as required.

It takes a commitment and resolve to take control of your life in the aftermath of a critical event. Having your world turned upside down can leave you feeling and thinking that you have lost all control. That control is re-established with each small step and subsequent victory.

The journey is made much easier with the support and encouragement of people who are like minded – that is, people who share your beliefs and the goals you have for yourself. Choosing your inner circle is critical.

I have observed that one of the most important strategies to thriving in the aftermath of bad things happening is to take control of what we say, how we say it, and who we say it to. Your mindset, perspective, or beliefs are directly connected to the words that come out of your mouth. Your words have a way of determining your future. From my experience, what you say repeatedly manifests itself in your reality.

Speaking life-giving words to enhance your mental and emotional well-being can be every bit as difficult as getting to the gym to enhance your physical well-being.

Regardless of the arena (physical, mental, emotional, behavioral, or spiritual), success in developing strong positive habits requires discipline, determination, and dedication.

Surrounding yourself with people who will both encourage and model life giving and positive conversations and interactions can make all the difference, especially if this perspective moves a hurting person outside of their normal disposition (cup half full versus cup half empty). If radical change is necessary, radical action may be vital, particularly when life and death hang in the balance. Doing the hard work can extend life, but perhaps even more importantly, it can enhance the quality of life for however long that may be – that's the real benefit.

Taking control of your life will involve the things that make you – you. You will not find a script, or a detailed to-do list, that will get you through the storm. What will get you through the storm is having an understanding of the principles for healthy and resilient living. The predictors of long term health are being relationally grounded, socially grounded, recreationally grounded, and spiritually grounded. Any support offered and any work done to establish these will enhance the quality of life during the recovery process and beyond.

CHAPTER 11 –
Embracing the New You

It is often stated that life is a journey. That journey, however, is comprised of experience after experience. The decisions we make following significant events determine whether the events ultimately propel us forward or paralyze us, recycling through the same pointless exercises. In our home, the following words are often repeated, particularly in the midst of a storm: "We will live from strength to strength."

Events in life create opportunities. It is what we choose to do with those opportunities that shape who we are. It is what we do with those opportunities that open and/or close the doors to our future.

I do not believe that everything happens for a reason. I believe that to a large extent, our lives are shaped by our choices and by how we choose to respond to the circumstances that are beyond our control.

Human history contains story after story of those who have pressed through and overcome challenges. Nelson Mandela, holocaust survivors, and many of those living out the aftermath of 911 are just a handful of many thousands who have pressed through the challenges they faced. It is impossible to truly understand or describe what they went through. What they all share is the tenacity, perseverance, commitment, and determination to make something good come from something very bad.

I know no greater example of someone embracing the new you than my grandfather. My grandfather was born in 1900 and would have turned ninety-two on October 30th, 1992 - the day my son was born. Our relationship was changed because of the events of that morning on October 23rd, 1963. Changed in a good way. It often seems that a tragedy is made more tragic when the victim is a child. As a parent, nothing is worse than seeing your children hurt. My grandfather was a loving man who cared deeply about people. This was why he dedicated so much of his life to the church where he served as a lay-pastor. Having me, his grandson, seriously injured on his watch could not have been easy.

My grandfather's life had been anything but easy. His early adult life was marked by tragedy, a word that in itself doesn't seem adequate to describe his experience. He had been born into a life of privilege, on a 3600-acre estate; one of three farms owned by his family. But war has a way of leveling the field. By that time his Mennonite faith had deep roots, which guided him to the decision to become a conscientious objector. While he survived the Bolshevik Revolution, he was not spared the brutalities of the conflict. While he was exposed to many horrific events, none would compare with events of October 30th, 1919, a day that should have been set aside to celebrate his birthday.

On October 30th, 1919 a group of bandits, known as the Machnow group, were roaming the countryside looting and killing, and came upon his family's estate. Because his father was unable to produce the 50,000 Rubles (equivalent to $12,500.00 at the time) they demanded, both his mother and father were shot. His mother was killed instantly while his father eventually died from the gunshot wounds twenty-eight hours later. These horrific events could have so easily destroyed my grandfather.

While my grandfather did not often speak of his early childhood, his formative years or his experiences as a young adult, their effect on his character was apparent. The resolve of his faith, his moral fabric, and the peace and joy that defined him were not compromised by his loss. My grandfather survived more than his share of bad things. My burns and my scars, were not his fault. No one would suggest otherwise. Too often, however, people carry a heavy burden of misplaced anger, blame and shame that creates resentment and bitterness in relationships that are needed most in times of loss.

While I was only four years old and oblivious to a lot of what happened in the aftermath of the fire, I recall clearly the warmth, tenderness, and love that was shared between my mother and my grandfather in the years that followed. That can only happen when, in the aftermath of bad things happening, people work through the tough stuff; extending grace rather than assigning blame.

What working through a crisis looks like will vary for every individual, but I would hope that this book will provide both a greater understanding of the natural responses that follow loss and tragedy, and how to encourage resiliency.

My grandfather was resilient, as was my mother, and I believe it was their demonstrated capacity for resiliency that encouraged me to also be resilient in the face of hardship. It is through our resilience that we are changed for the good, even when bad things happen. Embracing those changes is what embracing the new you is all about.

Those same traits can be used to describe anyone who has experienced a significant loss and pressed through the challenges that only they can describe because their stories are as unique as mine, and as unique as yours.

I look at the life that I have forged out of the circumstances of my life and I am overcome with emotion because I enjoy a blessed and incredible life. Embracing the you that you have become is not in any way minimizing the loss or tragic circumstances of the past. It is simply a reflection that you did not get stuck there or become paralyzed. It is a reflection that you have risen above your circumstances and refused to give up or accept a life of a being a victim.

Whether you are in the midst of a challenging season of loss or whether someone in your life has experienced a significant loss or change, let this be a time where you discover another layer to how we are all created. As leaders, we all possess the ability to encourage resiliency in others and knowing what to say and when to say it can help move people in the right direction.

We are continuing to evolve through every situation, circumstance, and interaction. It is my hope that as you continue to do the work, sometimes taking the path of most resistance, you will experience greater joy, increased satisfaction, and fulfillment in your relationships and all that you put your hands to.

APPENDIX A

I will reiterate that it is not my intention to proselytize to anyone but rather to provide the spiritual journey that I undertook when faced with the series of life-changing events.

I have always believed in God. I was raised in, by today's standards, a conservative Christian home. Our family attended church every Sunday, and family devotions took place daily before breakfast. It made for an early morning routine, but it was the only life I knew. While my faith has always been an important part of who I am, it became more personal and real to me during my battle with cancer. Too often a crisis leaves people asking the why me question. Sometimes people become angry with God for allowing bad things to happen, or worse yet, mad at God for directing bad things to happen because it is part of some greater plan God has designed for their life.

Despite all the Sundays I had spent in church, I found myself searching for answers. I was not looking for answers to the why me question, but answers to the 'what do I do now' question. I wasn't satisfied to sit back and let the events unfold with a que sera sera attitude. I could not find peace in the religious response of my experience being a part of God's plan. That was never the picture I had of God. My spirit resonated with a very different picture of God, one that I would discover is summarized in John 10:10 (Amplified Bible Translation): "A thief comes only to steal and kill and destroy. I came that they may have and enjoy real life, and have it in abundance, to the full, til it overflows." Those words resonated with me and allowed me to see God as a partner in my challenges, a God that I could embrace. It was certainly better than believing in a God that was either silent and uncaring, or worse yet, a God that was responsible for my circumstances. If any of that were true, it would be easy to understand the anger, confusion, or betrayal so often seen in the aftermath when bad things happen to people who believe in God.

Despite my family upbringing and my exposure to Godly teaching, I did not grow up with a faith framework of healing or miracles, something I so suddenly and desperately needed. I was raised in a conservative, Mennonite Christian home where teachings centered on strong moral values. These values determined what was an acceptable way to live and what was not. I lacked the understanding and spiritual weapons to engage in the biggest battle of my life.

I discovered that God has a way of finding us in our hour of need, especially when we are searching for truth.

There are many great teachers and resources available. Shortly after my diagnosis, I was blessed by people in my life who pointed me towards these teachers, resources, and the answers I was looking for.

A teaching void was filled when we began attending Springs Church.[7] Pastor Leon Fontaine[8] unashamedly teaches on healing in a way that challenged my traditional religious upbringing.

That teaching void was also filled with resources from around the world, much like how my physicians charted out my treatment plan. The never-been-seen presentation of leukemia left my physicians in unchartered waters. The Internet was used to reach out to cancer centers throughout North America for recommendations and what would have been considered best practices.

I had a great team looking after my care and the physicians and nursing staff, including the orderlies, will always have a special place in my heart.

Technology is a wonderful thing and gave us the opportunity to connect with spiritual resources around the world as well. You might say that after my diagnosis I began an international journey that would connect me with Godly men and women from all parts of this world.

---

7   Spring Church – A Spirit Contemporary church with locations in Winnipeg, Winnipeg Inner-City, Steinbach, and Selkirk, in Manitoba, Calgary Alberta, as well as Online.

8   Pastor Leon Fontaine is the Senior Pastor of Springs Church and the CEO of the Miracle Channel based in Lethbridge, Alberta, Canada.

Those men and women changed my life more than anything else, including the tragedies that marked my past and present circumstances. The result was a totally new understanding of God, His Word, and what it means to live by faith.

In my pursuit, I discovered that we are to live by faith (Habakkak 2:4; Romans 1:17; Galatians 3:11; Hebrews 10:38). These verses say that 'the just' shall live a certain way - by faith. If I was to live by faith, if my life was to be conducted in that particular way, I needed to know what that meant. How did living by faith impact what I needed to do on a day to day basis?

As a crime scene investigator, my world centered around evidence. It was no wonder the following verse resonated so well with me. Hebrews 11:1 (New King James Version) "Now faith is the substance of things hoped for, the evidence of things not seen." Faith is THE substance. It is the substance of things; the substance of physical things; the substance of spiritual things; the substance of seeing things; the substance of unseen things.

If faith is the substance of things and God made all things, then God had to use faith when he made all things. He had to use faith material.

Genesis 1 gives the account of creation and in verse 31 it is recorded that God saw everything that He had made. How was He making everything He saw? He was saying words; words that were filled with faith material.

I cannot count the number of times I have heard the phrase 'self-fulfilling prophecy' in reference to people predicting their own futures. People seem to have no problem speaking negative things about themselves and their futures, complaining really, about their circumstances and the unlikelihood things will ever improve. But if you flip the coin, people who speak positive things about themselves and their futures, even when their circumstances are far from positive, well, that usually raises a few eyebrows.

But that is exactly what it means to live by faith. John 1:1 (NKJV) says, "In the beginning was the Word, and the Word was with God, and the Word was God." God made the Word equal with Himself. What is the common denominator found in the Word of God and God Himself? The answer is faith material. The same faith that's in the heart of God is the faith that's in His Word. So let the Word of God equal faith.

That gives greater meaning to how we are to live – the just shall live by "the Word of God." Now I know how to live. I live by the Word of God. If I am going to be healed by faith, I need to be able to tell you the scriptures that I am standing on that will be responsible for my faith. The Word of God became my evidence that I was going to survive my battle with cancer, despite what the doctors were initially reporting to me.

Hebrews 11:1 became critical to my understanding and my resolve to not give up the fight for my healing. "Now the Word of God is the substance of things hoped for, and the Word of God is the evidence of things not seen." When you have evidence of something, that is proof that it really exists. You may not be able to see it, you may not know where it is, but you have the evidence that it exists. I was told that I had less than a two percent chance of survival – the initial medical reports were not good, but I had the evidence that my healing and full recovery was just a matter of time.

I finally understood the purpose of God's Word. God's Word is the manual of how we are to live our life. And it does have relevance for everyday.

In my reading, however, I recognized that like every promise in the Word, the blessings are always tied to a decision and action that is required on my part. The responsibilities are placed right back on me. If it's not working, I can't look at God as if it's his fault. That would be the misplaced anger towards God that I mentioned earlier. This is the foundation of our relationship with our Heavenly Father; a relationship based on our free will, a choice, that rests solely within each and every one of us.

In Matthew 6:33 (NKJV) it says, "Seek ye first the Kingdom of God and His righteousness and all these things that you need shall be added unto you." But how can we seek the Kingdom of God when we don't know what it is or where it is? The Amplified Bible translation offers some added text to enhance our understanding, "Seek ye first the Kingdom of God, God's way of doing, and being right and all these things shall be added unto you." Seek ye first God's way of doing.

In Mark 10:23 (NKJV) it says, "Then Jesus looked around and said to His disciples, How hard is it for those that have riches to enter into the Kingdom of God (*God's way of doing things*)?" And again in John 3:3 (King James Version), "Except a man be born again he cannot see the Kingdom of God *(God's way of doing things)*." So what does it look like to do things God's way? What is 'God's way of doing things?'

In Genesis 1:26 (KJV) it states, "And God said let us make man in our image after our likeness and let them have dominion." He said, "Take dominion, take authority." Then in verse 29 He said, "Behold I have given you every herb bearing seed which is upon the face of all the earth, and every tree, in which is the fruit of a tree yielding seed; to you it shall be for meat and sustenance." God gave man dominion/authority and seed.

In Genesis 8:22 (AMP) "While the earth remains, seedtime and harvest, cold and heat, summer and winter, and day and night shall not cease." God's way of doing everything that he does is <u>seedtime and harvest time</u>. Nothing just happens.

If you begin to put all these pieces together you get a better understanding of what "God's way of doing things" is. Inserting "God's way of doing things" into Matthew 6: "Seek ye first, God's way of doing, which is seed time and harvest time." In other words, "Seek ye first, seed time and harvest time and all these things that you need will be added to you."

The challenge is to treat your faith as a seed. How do you treat a seed? You plant it. And once you have planted it, you water it. Then you make sure to keep out all the weeds and make sure the insects don't come and destroy it. You do all that's necessary to nourish and protect that seed until the harvest comes. You care for it.

This is critical to experiencing your faith harvest. You have to take your faith seed, which is the Word of God, and treat it like you do any other seed and plant it. Where is the ground that will receive the Word of God seed? The Bible says the ground for this seed is the heart of man. The Word has to jump off the pages of the Bible and get into the ground called the heart.

There are three entrances into a man's heart: the eyes, ears, and mouth. Whatever you see, whatever you hear, whatever you speak is going to end up in your heart. The Bible says in Proverbs 4:23 (AMP) "Keep and guard your heart with all vigilance and above all that you guard, for out it flow the springs of life." You cannot guard your heart if you don't guard your eyes, guard your ears, and guard your mouth.

When I received that very bleak prognosis, I went to the Word of God and wrote down scriptures that talked about healing. I got all those scriptures together and then I went to work. I had my seed. But my seed did not produce until I treated it like a seed. So I planted it. I read the scriptures that I found on healing (planted in my heart through my eyes). I listened to teaching on healing by Gloria Copeland,[9] listened to the teaching of Creflow

---

9   Gloria Copeland serves alongside her husband Kenneth
      Copeland as part of the broader Kenneth Copeland Ministries
      located in Fort Worth, Texas, USA.

Dollar,[10] (planted in my heart through my ears). I confessed those scriptures over and over and over every day (planted in my heart through my mouth). I bombarded my heart with seed.

During the year it has taken to write this book, I will celebrate my nineteen-year anniversary of being cancer free. I have never been comfortable with the term remission because it just doesn't seem definitive enough. I am cancer free because I had amazing care and an amazing God and the cancer that had invaded by body was removed – all of it. And it's not coming back.

My new understanding of what it meant to live by faith had worked in the health arena, so I figured I may as well apply these principles to the next challenge that we were facing – the criminal trial of the man accused of murdering my mother-in-law Mary Buller.

I began bombarding my heart with His Word that related to justice. The story of Joshua and the walls of Jericho coming down found in Joshua, Chapter 6, came to me.

In the morning, before the court proceedings would begin, I would spend forty-five minutes to an hour walking around the courthouse (just like Joshua) declaring the truths about justice that I found in the Bible; that the truth and only the truth would be heard in the courtroom on that day. It became a part of my routine. I was

---

10 Dr. Creflo Dollar is the Senior Pastor of World Changers Church International located in College Park, Georgia, USA

bombarding my heart with His Word, reading it with my eyes, speaking it out loud with my mouth, and hearing it with my ears. When the jury returned a verdict of guilty on the first degree murder charge, it was the manifestation of the evidence that I had been holding onto for the entire legal proceedings.

In my search for answers to my 'God Questions' I discovered how to live. It changed my life and has impacted how I approach every situation that comes my way. It has given meaning to the Word of God. The Bible is no longer just a historical account from centuries ago. It is no longer important to spend time reading just because that would make me a good Christian. It redefined the relationship I have with Jesus Christ and my Heavenly Father and redefined the relevance of His Word.

It is a way of living that leads to the joy, peace, and confidence that can be our experience, even when we face the challenges that life brings.

Printed in Canada